BE YOUR BEST
MOTIVATOR
. . . AND BEYOND

Frances Coombes

Q·LEARNING

For UK orders: please contact Bookpoint Ltd, 130 Milton Park, Abingdon, Oxon OX14 4SB. Telephone: +44 (0) 1235 827720. Fax: +44 (0) 1235 400454. Lines are open 09.00–18.00, Monday to Saturday, with a 24-hour message answering service. You can also order through our website www.madaboutbooks.co.uk

British Library Cataloguing in Publication Data A catalogue record for this title is available from The British Library.

This edition, first published in UK 2003 by Hodder Headline Plc, 338 Euston Road, London NW1 3BH

Typeset by Servis Filmsetting Ltd, Manchester, England
Printed in Great Britain for Hodder & Stoughton Educational, a Division of Hodder Headline Plc, 338 Euston Road, London NW1 3BH by Cox & Wyman Ltd, Reading, Berkshire.

Impression number   10 9 8 7 6 5 4 3 2 1
Year   2007 2006 2005 2004 2003

Contents

Series Introduction

Perhaps you have had an idea, or wanted to achieve something, but known that you not only need some skills but also help with taking the risk and doing it for real. Maybe you have thought 'it is easy for him/her but not for me . . .'

This series is written for people who haven't got the time (or money) to attend a long training course or who are not lucky enough to be managed and mentored by a star in the field in which they want to succeed. These books will be 'back pocket' resources that will inspire and give practical tips that you can read up on and use in the next few minutes. They will also help you feel confident in taking skills that you already have into new situations at work, home and the community.

Lesley Gosling
Q. Learning

Introduction: Motivator

The most valuable gift that you can give yourelf is that of seeing yourself as a motivated, dynamic and successful person. One who constantly gets good ideas, structures the best ones, and then takes the necessary actions to make future goals happen. First come the thoughts, then the ideas, and these lead to the actions that make wishes reality.

The second most important ingredient to success is to hold a good image of your own world or environment: one in which everything comes together and works, rather than needing fixing.

Combine these two key elements with a passion and enthusiasm for the things you want to achieve and you have the main motivational ingredients necessary to make almost anything you desire happen.

Motivator is an inspirational yet highly practical book aimed at helping you generate creative ideas, structure your thinking and tap into your own motivational drivers to enable you to hasten the speed at which you reach your goals. It offers simple yet effective techniques to help you think more imaginatively about overcoming challenges in any situation. Each chapter focuses on honing particular success-making skills: thus improving your insight into situations and increasing your all-round performance. The book includes lots of sound information from motivational trainers, entrepreneurs and people responsible for making things happen.

Frances Coombes is a freelance journalist in the careers, sales, business and personal development fields. She has contributed regularly to business magazines and the *London Evening Standard*'s 'Just the Job' section covering work and self-development related training events, and writing features and interviews. She has trained with, interviewed and been motivated and inspired by some of the most powerful motivational trainers alive. She is also a master practitioner of Neuro-Linguistic Programming.

introduction

CHAPTER 1
Be Your Best Motivator.

◎ Do you feel that you would gain more from your efforts if all your energies flowed in the same direction towards your goals?

◎ Would you like greater confidence to take up new opportunities that move you beyond your current boundaries?

◎ Could you achieve more if you knew how to communicate more fully with people around you in work, at home in life?

Why not spend some time discovering how best to motivate yourself to get the results you want?

WHAT IS MOTIVATION?

The ancestor of every action is a thought.

RALPH WALDO EMERSON

Every business deal that is put together, love affair that blossoms, sporting game played or award struggled for and won, started out as nothing more than ideas with intentions in determined people's minds. There is a particular way of thinking which, when combined with purposeful actions, can achieve phenomenal results.

Motivation is a state of mind, an attitude, a way of thinking, being and doing that can reap you rewards beyond your wildest dreams. Just as preparing for a team sport or getting ready for a first date requires you to think tactically and become aware of how other players may engage, becoming highly motivated requires you to develop new skills and a new sense of awareness that wasn't necessarily present in your less ambitious state.

The greatest revolution of our generation is the discovery that human beings, by changing the inner attitudes of their minds, can change the outer aspects of their lives.

WILLIAM JAMES

Objects you see all around you from the clothes you wear, the chair you sit in, the light you read by – extending as far as unmanned space probes circuiting Mars – were all ideas conceived by people who felt passionate and purposeful enough to act upon and turn their thoughts into reality.

You were highly motivated as a toddler when, with a little encouragement, you taught yourself to walk, talk, discover the world and enjoy doing new things. Imagine how determined you were to urge your small body to repeatedly cling on to surfaces in your efforts to stand. You may have suffered knocks and shed tears of frustration. But your sense of curiosity was aroused and the only way you could find out what was happening beyond your boundaries was to walk – so you did it.

People who do not allow themselves to imagine purposeful actions that they could take to achieve their desires are often unfulfilled because they kill their unborn dreams. If you are unaware of a way to achieve a desired outcome, you won't even aim for it. It is a case of 'Don't set your sights too high and you won't be disappointed.' However, you won't be happy either.

Do what you love and success will come easily

If you have not examined where the edges of your achievement boundaries might be lately, here is a chance to explore afresh, bringing with you the same elements of curiosity and excitement you once possessed as a toddler. Who knows what will happen when you step to the edges of your boundaries and beyond – you may be able to soar.

WHAT IF . . . IMAGINE THE FUTURE . . . AND ALLOW YOURSELF TO DREAM

> Success is not the result of spontaneous combustion. You must set yourself on fire.
>
> REGGIE LEACH

In the film *South Pacific* there is a song which goes 'happy talking talking, happy talk, talk about things you'd like to do. You've got to have a dream, if you don't have a dream – how you gonna have a dream come true?' Have you got a dream you'd like to turn into a dream come true? Have you got 20 minutes to engage in a happy talking plan?

WHAT DO YOU WANT?

Knowing who you are and discovering what you really want is the key to taking actions that will propel you towards greater successes. What are the things that you are naturally drawn to? What are the changes you will need to make to get the life you want? People often say they know what they want and may spend their time engaged in displacement activities, only to find after they've swapped their job, partner or location that they've carried with them their feelings of discontent. They've changed what seemed obvious in their lives but have not identified the main changes that will make the difference to them.

When you know what you want and can see what is holding you back you can begin to solve any problems that might be keeping you locked away from exploring your success potential. One way to do this is to ask yourself lots of questions out loud. Human beings have evolved by solving puzzles; they are problem seeking missiles, designed to home-in and find answers once a question has been voiced.

Progress now

If you were absolutely certain that you would be wildly successful at everything you tried, what are the things you would most like to achieve? Spend 20 minutes and write a list.

- Your ideas are mind seeds so choose the ones that truly excite you and are most likely to flourish.

- Ask yourself 'What things do I really love doing?' 'What do I feel really excited and enlivened about?'

- When you know what inspires you, the sort of venture that you want to give yourself completely to, the next step is find out how to make money at it. Who do you know or have you read about who is already engaged in the sort of venture you want to explore?

- Some goal-driven people seek only results but don't enjoy the process of getting to them. Make sure you really will enjoy engaging in your endeavours but also take some time out to connect to other people and smell the flowers along your route to success.

CASE STUDY

Entrepreneur and motivational speaker Peter Thomson of Peter
Thomson International Plc is a very motivated person and he
lives by the questions he asks himself. Peter finished college with
few 'O' levels and little money and went on to create three
successful businesses. His first business became the largest tracing
agency in Europe within two years of opening, and the last he
sold after five years for £4.2 million.

Peter believes that self-questioning is vital and says that he lives by
the questions he asks himself each day. He thinks that the reason
many people do not succeed in business is because they do not
ask themselves the hard questions you need to answer before you
can get results. He says, 'People often say I'd do anything for
"your lifestyle" or "the amount of money" or "free time" you have
– but they wouldn't. When I ask them "What stops you then?"
they say they don't have time.'

He says, 'The easy questions are "What shall I watch on TV
tonight?" or "Shall I have a take-away dinner?" The hard questions
are the ones that when you look in the mirror you have to give an
honest answer to. I live by the questions I ask myself every single
day. Questions such as "What skills do I have that will tie in with
the things I want in life" and "How do I leverage it?" Having
questions like these constantly in mind has enabled Peter to pull
off achievements that many people can only dream about.

(7)

Progress now

Peter says, 'Here's a hard question – "How do I double my income in a year? Spend ten minutes asking yourself this question each morning for seven days and list the ideas you come up with. Force yourself to think about the skills you possess and how you can harness them to double your income by this date next year, and write down 20 answers. You will get many nuggets in there.'

People like Peter Thomson, who are motivated towards a goal, are far more likely to achieve what they want in the areas they concentrate their efforts. Their bonus is that they feel more alive and in tune with what is going on than ordinary mortals, and they enjoy a sense of power that comes from knowing that they can positively make a difference, for themselves and for others.

Being motivated is the nearest thing to magic you can achieve because it develops a 'can do' attitude. This is the most critical accessory to success in any endeavour. Anyone who experiences being totally motivated and achieving his or her goals on a regular basis may find it hard to understand the person who settles for dawdling through life and accepting whatever fate or the result of their inaction chooses to deal them. Let's start thinking about the changes you want to make.

Progress now

Develop a habit of questioning. If you are starting out on the path of self-discovery, here are some questions to ask yourself. Spend 20 minutes listing your answers and don't censor yourself – just get everything down.

- What things do I enjoy doing?
- What am I good at?
- What, seriously, do I want out of life?
- What are the things I could do to get this?
- What is the price I would have to pay to get this?
- Am I willing to pay the price?

TRANSITIONS, WHY NOW?

What are your reasons for wanting to change and move on from where you are now? There may be some small niggles and worries that can be adjusted and put right, others may be hanging around your neck like an albatross.

People say there is nothing so powerful as an idea whose time has come – but how do you know that your time for change has come? It may have come and gone, or not arrived yet.

> A lot of people make their changes when the pain of staying at the place they're at becomes greater than the fear of moving on and stepping into an uncertain future.
>
> GREGG LEVOY, MOTIVATIONAL SPEAKER

Below are some of the reasons that people have given for why they decided to make changes in their lives.

Vic Taylor, a further education teacher, was 49 when he was made redundant. He now runs MyNewt Enterprises, a one-person, environmental roadshow for children. He says: 'I created this job because I needed the money. I felt I was too old for anyone to want to employ me, so I sat down and planned my future. I enjoy it so much I wish I'd done it earlier.'

- Marco Pierre White, restaurateur, put his ambition down to watching his talented but cautious father's behaviour. 'He was ambitious but could not bring himself to take a risk or dare, and had to live his life knowing he had never reached his potential,' says Pierre. 'His failure was an important lesson for me.'

- Patrick Curzon, a bank manager: 'I just keep thinking there must be more to life than working in a bank. Patrick decided to become self-employed and run his own income tax returns franchise. 'My greatest fears were of giving up the security of a regular paycheck and the fact that I might fail at the business.' Two years ago he started the change and decreased his working days at the bank from five gradually down to two days a week as his business grew. Patrick has recently taken on new premises and two staff and decided he will quit the bank within the next six months.

Success is doing – not wishing!

One of the most powerful questions anyone who wants to start achieving can ask themselves each day is, 'What are the most important things I can do today to take me nearer to my goals?' then, and this is important, they follow through with actions. Initially it might be:

- A telephone call to find out more about something.
- Looking for books or ideas about someone who has done similar things.
- A plan of action.
- Sorting out your skills and abilities.
- Attending seminars and workshops.
- Finding and talking to people who share your dreams.
- Looking for the next step to take that leads towards your goals.

Progress now

Imagine yourself at the end of your life looking back at your past achievements. What dreams and goals do you most regret never having fulfilled? List them and ask yourself, how many of them are realistic and achievable, and of those that are, ask: 'If I was actively working on this goal, what would be the next actions that I would be taking today to propel me towards it?'

If you want some practice, and already have a goal in mind, write down the next six actions you will take today to move you towards your outcome. Use any of the methods above, along with ideas of your own. Decide that you will take six more follow-on actions each day for 20 days, and at the end of that time review your progress to see whether your goal seems more achievable now. After 21 days you may have discarded your original idea for something completely different. How does your dream look to you now? Is it further away in the distance or does it seem any closer?

Progress now

Think of three people you know who you feel are capable of much more than whatever job or role they play in life. Then list any limiting beliefs you hear them repeat about their abilities to reinforce their negative beliefs, i.e. 'It's too difficult for me', 'I'll never get a look in'. Do you have any limiting beliefs that might be holding you back from achieving success? Write your limiting beliefs down so that you can look at ways to change them to beliefs that will support your aims.

WHATEVER YOU BELIEVE ABOUT YOURSELF IS TRUE FOR YOU

Do you know people who hold beliefs about themselves or their abilities that undermine them? What types of thing do you hear them say about themselves that reinforce their beliefs? Have they chosen partners or friends who reinforce these ideas for them?

Have you challenged any of the beliefs that you have carried with you for a long time? Beliefs that may get in the way of our achievements could include:

- I'm stupid/scatterbrained/incompetent/not clever enough.
- People like me don't run successful businesses/achieve success.
- I don't deserve it.
- I'm too old/too young/unqualified/don't know how to do it.

If you believe you can, or if you believe you can't – you are probably right.

HENRY FORD

14

GETTING RID OF LIMITING BELIEFS

Now here's a limiting belief – 'I can't change'. Another one is: 'It's always been done like this', which implies that something cannot be changed because it has always been the same. Changing your thoughts, behaviours and beliefs one at a time and in small ways is often all that is needed to begin to change your limiting beliefs and to start steering your life to go in a direction that brings success.

Your beliefs are not carved in stone; you are constantly changing them throughout your life based on the incoming information you receive. Can you recall the first time someone told you that Father Christmas was not real? What did you do? Most children carry on believing until overwhelming evidence triggers disbelief. Child star Shirley Temple said she stopped believing in Santa Claus when she was taken to a department store to meet him and he asked her for her autograph. What other major beliefs have you changed over time?

How do you change beliefs?

How do untidy children, who turn into untidy adolescents, and then tidy adults (well most of them) make that transition? They change their beliefs about tidiness.

An untidy person who wants to tidy up their mess but holds the belief 'I don't know how to tidy up' or 'Someone else will do it' will find their progress to be tidy inhibited. Often simply changing their thinking to be more enabling such as: 'I am not the sort of person who leaves my mess around for other people to clear up' or 'I take responsibility for my actions and take control of my environment' will be the catalyst that launches them into becoming a tidy person.

Initially you might not know what actions lead to 'tidy' but you have started a chain of thinking events and your brain looks around for comparisons.

People hold beliefs about all sorts of things: Father Christmas, tidiness, religion, work, politics and their own capabilities. Once these beliefs are established, we may never challenge them again, unless there is overwhelming evidence to do so.

Presuppositions are the beliefs that individuals hold about themselves or others or about how they think things are in the world. We presuppose that these beliefs are true and act as if they are. At one time it was widely believed that the world was flat. If you held that belief now, how would it affect your thoughts on travelling to the underside of the world – say Australia? A widely shared belief at present is that the world is round, when to physicists it is not completely round. However, enough of us share the belief to make it appear true and so we talk of travelling around the world.

Progress now

Think of an action that you once believed you couldn't do, but can do now, for instance, riding a bike, roller-skating, swimming, giving a talk, chairing a meeting. How did you feel before you performed the feat? Did you think you would ever do it? What happened to change your thinking from 'I can't do that' to 'I can do that!'

Now think of something you cannot do at present but would like to. Ask yourself some questions about the actions you need to be able to do to achieve it. People often think in absolutes, such as 'I can't do that . . .' Let's take something that you currently believe you cannot do and play with some new questioning to loosen up the language.

Present belief	New question
I can't do that . . .	What would happen if you could?
I can't do that <u>yet</u>	What <u>will</u> happen when you <u>can</u>?

Changing your language and moving from 'I can't do that' (an absolute) to 'I can't do that yet' (which presupposes that you can see a time in the future when you can), offers a glimmer of hope. Having freed up the questions a little, imagine in detail having performed the action and answer this question:

What did I do differently, or what was different about me, that enabled me to do it?

The human brain processes both fact and imagined events as real. That is why you can imagine something sad, make an association and start crying, even though you have not experienced the event. In this case your brain may have imagined you were riding a bike, even though you do not yet know how to. You have asked it a question about how you did that and, even though the experience was not real, it will give you the answer you require with all the steps you took and how and at what point your feelings and beliefs changed in order to perform the task. For someone else who does the same task the process might be different.

Try some more questions you can put to yourself about your capabilities. You might believe 'I can't give a presentation in front of people.'

Present belief	New question
It's too difficult	What would have to happen to you for it to be easier?

(If you listen your brain will tell what you need in order to make the action seem easier.)

It's easier now but . . .	and what else would you need to have or do to make it even easier than that?

Remembering when – Celebrate your achievements

Have you ever performed a task incredibly well, so well you thought it was magic? It may have been in school performing a sport, persuading a group of work colleagues to agree to your plan, being heard in difficult circumstances, making a sale to a particularly difficult customer or asking someone for a date. Perhaps you imagined beforehand that you were already in the situation seeing the events as they unfolded, hearing the sounds of surprise, excitement or enjoyment from the others involved, seeing their faces become more animated, and feeling the sorts of feelings that you experienced in the actual situations.

When the event occurred, did it feel as if you were playing your part with ease? Had you mentally prepared for the event and rehearsed it in your mind? Were you purposeful in your thoughts, beliefs and behaviour, and if so, were the people you were interacting with aware of this?

Our behaviour stems from our beliefs. In the above instance you believed in yourself and that you would do whatever you set out to do. The vision of your success is stored in your mind and body, and you can imagine the event by playing it back in your mind. You may see the event in colour, like watching a movie, and recall each frame in sequence. In your body you may feel the same feelings you felt in synchronicity with the events you saw.

Here is an interesting question to put to yourself: If you took all your past memories and images of success and the bright pictures and strong emotional feelings that are tied up with them and carried these types of beliefs about your capabilities into the future – what sorts of feats might you be able to achieve if you knew you just could not fail?

MOVING FROM THINKING TO DOING

This book will help you to move from just thinking about things you would like to achieve to actually doing them. The action plan has ten major steps offering tools, tips and techniques for becoming more motivated, with advice from experts and motivational speakers to nudge you on your way. People's thinking styles are examined and we look at ways of communicating your requests to different types of thinkers in ways which are more meaningful to them.

The motivational skills wheel

Below are some of the main skills that successful people either have or work hard towards achieving:

1. Motivating yourself to do things.
2. Visualization – the future. What you want, what does better look like? Harnessing the power of emotions.
3. Feeling purposeful – can you remember the feeling and describe it in a particular situation and explain how you felt? Do you know how to align your beliefs and values to your purpose?
4. Goal setting – do you know how to create well-formed goals?
5. Getting rid of procrastination. In life, in work – do you know how to motivate yourself into action?
6. Communication skills – how good are you at interpersonal skills and understanding how to motivate other people?
7. Challenging limiting beliefs that hold you back. How good are you at challenging limiting beliefs that may be holding you back?
8. Taking risks to move on. Do you have a strategy? Are you prepared to take risks to move closer to your goals?
9. Modelling – what have you learned from observing successful people's behaviour and its practical applications?
10. Time management. How good are you at working within time frames and putting things all together?

THE MOTIVATIONAL WHEEL – BUILDING YOUR SKILLS AND ABILITIES

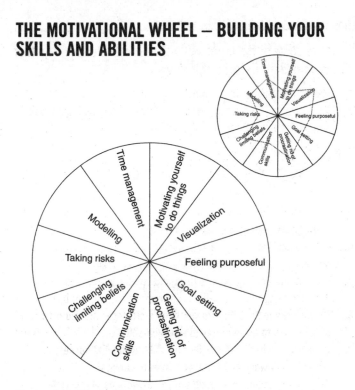

Figure 1.1 The motivational wheel

Imagine each spoke of the wheel represents a skill or ability that motivated people are accomplished at. How do you rate your level of competency under each of the headings on a scale of 1 to 10? Number 1 represents the middle of the wheel and 10 the outer rim. Now draw a dot on each of the spokes at the competency level you think you presently operate at in each of the ten skills. This is only a thumbnail sketch for your own benefit, so do not think deeply, do it quickly – draw your dots wherever you think they should be. Take a ruler and join the dots to their adjacent spokes. The result should resemble an uneven pointed star shape.

If you have high scores on all levels but have at least three areas that you feel you could improve on, say, Visualization, Communication skills, Modelling and Taking risks, then perhaps it is time to extend your boundaries in a controlled way.

What have you learned about yourself and your particular strengths and weaknesses from this overview of the ingredients that go towards your recipe for a highly motivated you?

YOUR BLUEPRINT FOR SUCCESS

You are now armed with your personal assessment of your skills and abilities. Remember, these are only beliefs that you hold about your competencies and may not be wholly accurate. If you are in a negative frame of mind, you may have scored yourself lower than on a day when you feel happy or confident – but it does not really matter. Like a visitor who takes a route map to travel on the subway, you now have an overview of the areas you wish to touch on in order to become a successful achiever in the shortest possible time. You can either choose to work on the areas that seem to need most improving first or read through the book and then decide what to do. It is up to you.

The experience should be enjoyable, so the action exercises are short, but designed to challenge and move you quickly to the next step of your journey towards your goals. By the time you fill in the motivation wheel again, towards the end of the book, you will find that your confidence has grown in several or maybe in all areas. That is really what motivation is about – having the confidence to act on your dreams.

SUMMARY

- An idea is only a notion unless an action follows.
- Asking yourself questions is crucial.
- Motivated people first find out what they truly want from life, then set out to get it.
- Constant learning, doing and skills enhancement are the tools of the motivation trade.

CHAPTER 2
Imagination – Rehearsing Your Dreams

- Do you know how to share your dreams with others?

- Would you like to have more of the creative ideas necessary to contribute towards your success?

- Do you need some help evaluating your ideas?

Imagination is the beginning of creation. You imagine what you desire; you will what you imagine; and at last you create what you will.

GEORGE BERNARD SHAW

'Dream it – then do it!' This may sound simplistic, but that is exactly how we determine our level of achievement. We dream about the things we want to achieve and then take the actions that propel us towards our goals. Your level of motivation is the key to success in every area of your life. The more frequently you see yourself getting the things you aim for, the more likely you are to get them and to picture yourself as a winner.

Being successful at reaching your goals is the biggest and most important gift you can give yourself. This chapter is about increasing your imaginative abilities to build strong visual images of what you want to achieve.

Good ideas do not only come to a few gifted people; they are free to anyone who is prepared to put their mind to work and imagine how they will create their dreams. They will calculate their odds of winning whatever they want to achieve; the types of skills and talents they will require to reach their goal and who they will need to help them on their way. The bigger the dream, the more likely it is that they will need to inspire other people to help them reach their goals.

BUILD A SHARED DREAM

Successful people in many fields use imaging. Effective leaders in industry, sport, politics and anywhere where team effort is required, seek to influence their teams by their actions and words. To successfully motivate others, they need to have energy and a good image of themselves as winners, and to convey the excitement and challenge of what they are doing to their workforce — the foot soldiers responsible for making success happen.

Motivators often define their aims by using a shared vision or metaphor of what it looks or feels like when they are engaged in the activity that makes them successful. This shorthand description of how their leader sees success enables team members to instantly recognize what it feels like when they are acting effectively in pursuit of team goals.

Here is part of an interview with a young and very successful businessman talking about his company. Notice that, as he talks, he also shares his visions of how he sees success.

INSPIRATIONAL VOICE

Thirty-four-year-old Neil Gandhi, vice president of sales at Attenda, a Web design company currently spearheading its way into Europe, has had a phenomenal success in selling. When asked why he was successful in business, he spread his hands high in the air in front of him and said, 'I believe it's all out there – you've just got to go out there and get it.'

At 21, Gandhi, recognized the potential for business-to-business mail order computer systems and set up his first company, Elite Computer Systems. By the age of 24, he had sold the company and moved to Wordperfect in a channel marketing role. Neil says, 'Wordperfect wanted someone with energy and the ability to make a deal, and I had that. I was responsible for £20 million revenues when I arrived and turnover was about £40 million when I left. The market was growing massively at the time, demand for Wordperfect was huge. Selling in a market that's going up is like riding a wave.

'The channel marketing role was all about having masses of energy and it worked perfectly for me. I created a pull-through, ensuring that our products were always in customers' thoughts. I spent each day on one of the huge sales floors with 200 telesales agents, motivating the salesforce to sell our products.'

Source: Courtesy of MPMG Ltd, *Sales Director Magazine.*
Copyright Frances Coombes

Notice how Neil sees success as something 'out there' – as if he can reach up and pluck it from the air. He uses a sporting metaphor to describe the way he feels success: 'it's like riding a wave'. Motivating 200 people on a sales floor is nothing like surfing waves, but he is giving us an insight into how he feels when he is doing something successfully. People tend to use descriptive language like this when they are describing events that are magical or are heightened experiences for them.

What you see repeatedly in your mind's eye is what you tend to get. If you see yourself as successful then you become it. However, imaging is not a substitute for action but a supplement to it. You can visualize yourself being a pop star or a world-class athlete, yet unless you also take the follow-through actions towards it, nothing is going to happen.

THE METAPHORS OF SUCCESS

If you want a snapshot of how a person sees the world, listen for the little personal metaphors they include when they describe an action, an event or the world as being like something else. This tells you what things feel like to them. Let's turn the spotlight on you and look at the descriptions you convey to yourself and other people about how you view your world. Do this quickly – it should take only a few seconds.

Progress now

Forrest Gump, in the film of that name (1994), said his mother always said that 'Life is like a box of chocolates. You never know what you are going to get next'. What is your shorthand metaphor for life? Very quickly and without thinking, finish the sentence with the first words that leap into your mind. 'Life is like . . .' Don't cheat, it's the first, not the second or third idea that came into your mind.

If you said life is like a 'battlefield' then we might assume that you see continual conflict in your life. People give all sorts of descriptions for this. Some see their world as being 'orchestrated by a conductor', 'one long holiday', 'a nightmare', 'like a roller coaster' or 'full of wonder'. These people could all share the same office but still have completely different ways of interpreting the incoming information they receive from their surroundings, based on how their individual models of the world work.

We experience life through five senses: what we see, hear, smell, feel and taste. Each person perceives the world and reality differently, according to how we absorb information, organize it into meaningful patterns and filter it in a way that is meaningful to us. We all use self-talk and imagery to describe what we think is happening around us. We look for and filter what we want to see and close down on what we do not want to see. For instance, have you noticed that if you have bought a particular type of car, suddenly you start to see lots of the same type of car, or if you have just had a baby you start to notice babies? There are not suddenly more cars or babies, but your brain is now screening for them. The effect of this type of information filtering is that you get more of what you expect to get.

Progress now

If you woke up tomorrow and decided to change your metaphor for life to just the way you wanted it to be, what would you change it to? Think quickly and don't censor. Just write it down and say it out loud – change it until you hear it and know it suits you. 'I would like my life to be like . . .'

Can you see how changing your metaphor for life from an image of a 'battlefield' to one of 'a place with unlimited opportunities' or 'full of friendly faces' could change how you view the world, connect to other people and how you make decisions in it?

Write some descriptions of what you are like when you are at your personal best, for example:

◊ When I'm doing what I'm good at, it's as easy as slicing butter with a hot knife.

◊ I make things happen by taking actions.

◊ If someone else can do it, so can I.

◊ To win more, I'm prepared to fail more.

CREATING GOOD IDEAS

Before you can make your visions a reality, you have to create some good ideas that align with the sorts of things that others want and which are currently in demand. We create our ideas by thinking about what often seem like problems and imagining how we might resolve them. Solutions usually come after people have done the necessary preparation and have gathered information around the subject.

If history is correct, then evolution does not seem to have changed our thinking processes or the way we get our creative breakthroughs. First, we have a problem to solve and we worry about it and think of all the possible permutations for solving it that we can. Then, when our mind is idling, we make the imaginative leaps that lead to a solution.

In the third century BC Archimedes had his 'eureka' moment while getting into the bath. The King of Syracuse, Hiero, asked him to find out if the newly commissioned royal crown was made of pure gold or had been substituted with a less valuable metal. As he relaxed and stepped into his bath, Archimedes noticed that his bodyweight displaced an exact amount of water and the idea struck him that a solid gold crown would have an exact weight as well. Archimedes was so thrilled by his discovery that he became the world's first documented streaker when he took to the streets shouting 'eureka'.

- On a warm afternoon in 1667, Sir Isaac Newton was sitting under the shade of some apple trees. He'd just eaten, had a few drinks and was feeling in a 'contemplative mood', when an apple fell to the ground and the notion of gravity first struck him.

- Kekule hit on his molecular architecture in 1858 as he relaxed and dozed in front of the fire. He dreamed of snakes made out of long rows of atoms. Suddenly one snake seized hold of its own tail and Kekule woke up with the beginning of the theory of the benzene ring.

In a recent study, 200 scientists were asked if a solution to a problem they were thinking about had ever just popped into their heads – nearly 85 per cent said 'Yes'. It usually happened when they were away from the problem.

When it comes to really brilliant ideas, it seems that purely rational thinking can only lead you so far. When you have collected and sifted all the relevant information, there comes a point when you deliberately need to distance yourself from the problem, switch off and wait for the imaginative leap. The imaginative leap is not just finding the solution to a problem, with it comes an unshakeable belief that something that could not be done before can now be done.

The secret is in the imagining – dream it then do it

Believing that something can be done sets the wheels in motion to find a way to achieve it. Until Roger Bannister ran the four-minute mile in 1954, nobody believed a human could possibly run so fast. Within months of Bannister having achieved his dream, several people broke the four-minute mile record – simply because they now had evidence that it could be done.

Do you have dreams that you would like to achieve that you presently think are impossible? Why not allow yourself some time to dream about them? Is it worth spending ten minutes to examine whether some of the things you secretly desire might just be achievable? After all, you have nothing to lose.

CHANGING BELIEFS FROM CAN'T TO CAN

🖉 If you have a skill even remotely linked to what you want to do, maybe one that could be developed, write it down.

🖉 If you are in a unique position to have knowledge about this skill, perhaps because it is in your workplace, write it down.

🖉 If you believe that you could achieve your aim if you believed you could more strongly, write it down.

🖉 If you know what would convince you that you could do it, write it down.

🖉 If you know people who might help you – it doesn't matter whether you think they would or not – write it down.

🖉 If you know some or all of the steps you would have to take to achieve your goal, write them down.

Has your thinking changed about reaching that goal? Do you feel in any way that your idea might be closer and more possible now? Sometimes people who do this exercise come up with a completely different idea from the one they worked on. Whatever you come up with, it is the right thing for you.

Most of our ideas are not new; they come from associating different aspects of products, inventions and ideas produced by other people and putting them together in a novel way. Often the environment that people work in can be a hotbed for creative, inventive and imaginative ideas because people on the shopfloor can see exactly what the problems are.

- Two RAF electricians, Martin Childs and Steve McBride, found a way to save the RAF £500,000 a year on time spent sucking out fuel from aircraft during routine maintenance. They found a way of reversing the aircraft's refuelling capability to suck out fuel by disconnecting only one wire in the aircraft's complex electrical system. Now, the once lengthy fuel-draining procedure on Tornado fighter bombers is completed in minutes.

- Philip Barnes-Warden, a uniform services' support manager with the Metropolitan Police, suggested recycling old police uniforms. The idea was taken onboard and now a recycling company provides a textile skip, and clothes are sent to developing countries or recycled into padding for the motor industry. In addition to the annual savings of £12,000 on skip hire, the Met receives £65 per ton from a recycling company for the clothing collected, which generates £6,500 a year.

The Ministry of Defence (MOD) are members of Ideas UK, an idea generating and staff recognition association, and run one of the most successful ideas generation schemes in Britain. The scheme attracts 2,500 ideas a year and generates staggering savings in the region of £20 million. Ideas range from ground-breaking technological improvements, such as a method of mapping the undersurface of the Arctic ice cap to allow submarines to navigate more effectively, to ideas that improve safety or the environment or simplify office procedures. Recent successes have included recycling water used to clean aircraft engines, saving 24 cubic metres of water (enough to fill 15 Olympic-sized swimming pools), the use of outsized nuts to protect vulnerable instruments from seat buckles when pilots unstrap themselves from Harrier jump jets, and increasing warehouse storage capacity and reducing costs by placing half-sized pallets under the roof apex. A saving of £3 million was made from one idea to adapt a commercial system to provide ship-to-shore communications for the Royal Navy.

David Follis runs the Ministry of Defence's 'GEMS ideas scheme' whose electricians came up with the fuel-draining procedure that saves the Royal Air Force £500,000 a year. He says that 'One reason regular savings like this are made is because staff are encouraged and given a framework to submit their ideas in. In fact all of the above ideas were harvested because of facilities made available to staff to submit their ideas.'

David also says that 'People can feel awkward about volunteering ideas, particularly at junior level, so an officially recognized scheme helps to give them confidence. We also make sure that staff have direct access to our scheme without having to route their ideas through their managers. Again this helps to overcome any natural inhibitions'. The key to any successful scheme is user-friendliness and the backing of top management. 'Without getting these two things right your ideas-generating scheme is pretty well doomed to failure' says David. The GEMS scheme is reviewed every two years, to take account of user feedback and to maintain its effectiveness.

If you had a brilliant idea about changing or finding a solution to a problem in work, how would you capture it and turn it into reality? We asked Andrew Wood, President of Ideas Management Inc. in Washington, DC, an ideas generation company that also helps organizations set up their own ideas-generation schemes, about how he goes about it. He says: 'If you create the right mind-set and the opportunity to listen, then people will generate

41

ideas. However, we need to try to get good quality ideas, and that may mean that to start with we have to accept imperfect ones. Most people do not actively observe and if they don't see the problem, they will also miss spotting the opportunity to solve it.

'Most great ideas came about because someone said "Why do we have to do it this way?" or "Wouldn't it be better if we did it this way?" When I work in companies helping employers set up workplace initiatives, I ask questions that make people notice things – often things that they have taken for granted for years. I also look for alternative solutions, sometimes by transposing things between locations and places by asking questions such as "How would an airline deal with queues (if we were a bank)?"

To make sure that great ideas do not slip through the net, you need a framework to get your ideas into a shape so that you can present them to interested parties. Start by brainstorming and asking yourself the questions in the 'Progress now' opposite.

Progress now

Write three sentences:

1. Detailing what the problem is.
2. How it has arisen.
3. What is your desired outcome?

Use these as headings to flesh out more detail under each. Then ask yourself questions, such as:

- Is a solution necessary?
- What will happen if things stay the same?
- What will solve the problem for me?
- How will my suggestion resolve the problem?

Draw diagrams or pictures that will help others to understand your idea more clearly. Estimate what the saving will be in time or money if the idea is implemented.

Although making a difference at work is important to many people, often the most satisfying achievements are through the type of work people create for themselves. Never underestimate the power of necessity – when it is backed up with a really good idea it can drive people to the sort of success that other people might feel is impossible.

In the early 1960s, Diana Mellor moved to London and needed to earn a living. She had a young baby to support and could not leave home. Diana had been a journalist in New Zealand and friends there would pass her name to travellers seeking work in London.

Diana says, 'I soon realized that secretaries from New Zealand were well trained and in demand.' She set up her temping agency working from a coin-box operated telephone in a hallway outside her flat, and Southern Cross Employment Agency was born. Diana has varied her business and now has the largest temping agency for dental assistants in London, placing hundreds of people in temporary jobs each week.

GETTING GOOD IDEAS – THE CREATIVE PROCESS

There are at least five stages to getting good ideas, although some people have many more.

1. First, you see the problem, need, aim or goal – you want to achieve something and you think about what you would like to do.

2. In stage two you investigate possibilities for developing the idea. You look at what went before, what might work and you imagine combinations of ideas to see what you can come up with.

3. Stage three is the incubation period where you put your sub-conscious to work. You may be doing something totally unrelated and relaxing like playing with the suds in the washing-up bowl, when suddenly stage four – the eureka moment – happens and you run out into the streets with your washing-up gloves on.

4. Illumination – the moment when you are suddenly struck by the answer. Often it is so simple you wonder why you didn't think of it before.

5. Stage five is where you put on your logical head again and seek verification of your hunches and insights. The brainstorming method that people use for coming up with workplace ideas can help with this (page 46).

There are three distinctive types of thinking involved in coming up with a good idea. These are

1. Uninhibited brainstorming to get the ideas. At this stage it is best to consider yourself to be the most knowledgeable person in the world and keep brainstorming for ideas.

2. Logical procedural thinking to see how things will work. You are testing the idea, looking for any obvious problems or oversights.

3. And then comes the critical thinking to get an overview of the sorts of things that could stop your idea from being a winner.

Brainstorming is probably the most enjoyable part of idea generation, once you get the hang of it. When you are brainstorming ideas it is important not to limit yourself in any way by being critical or negative about the ideas you think of.

If you feel your brain could do with a workout to become more imaginative at making connections between unrelated objects then try the following exercise. Each morning for a month practise building your ability to force relationships on unrelated objects. If you do this you will get even better at thinking of bright ideas.

Progress now

Spend ten minutes a day to increase your ability to think creatively about the different ways in which everyday objects can be used. Time yourself and aim to come up with at least 30 things to do with each object, say a brick, a bin-lid, a wheel, a paper bag, a dinner plate. Pick a new object each day.

SCORING: Below 10 – poor, unimaginative. 10–15 you are getting better. 15–20 good. 20–25 congratulations, you are really motoring. 25–30 you are a genius.

Once you have high scores for uses with single associations, move on to combining two and then three unassociated objects. When your brain is really buzzing, start working on a solution to your own particular challenge.

Progress now

Start imagining your own solutions. Imagine that the current problem you want a solution to has already been solved. What would the answer be? Ask yourself what things you would have needed to do to achieve this? What type of tools, skills or people would you need to have access to? Draw a picture – an abstract will suffice – of the solution. Sometimes this will be enough information to send your imagination into 'new ideas' mode.

An idea is only a notion – unless an action follows

It is helpful, once you begin flexing your mental muscles and getting lots of ideas, to immediately follow up with feasible actions so that you get used to achieving the things you want to on a regular basis. Start with small tasks first and work your way up. Each small success will reinforce your self-belief as a winner. Begin to notice and eliminate negative thoughts you may have when building your dreams, such as 'it's impossible' and 'I can't'. Even accidentally triggered thoughts of 'it's impossible' can set of a chain reaction of other negative thoughts designed to prove you right.

TRUSTING YOUR INTUITION

Being imaginative, chasing information and accumulating skills and knowledge may not be enough to make you a winner unless you also learn to listen to and trust your instincts. Weston Agor, a lecturer at the University of Texas, gave 2,000 managers a test used to assess their personality traits. He found that, without exception, senior executives scored higher than middle managers when it came to thinking intuitively.

Successful business negotiators tend to weigh up a situation logically but they also listen to their hunches.

Primitive humans, whose lifestyle and physical survival depended on instinctive knowing and the ability to tune into animal behaviour patterns, weather and other subtle changes, were more attuned to picking up subliminal messages. In order to stay alive they depended on following their hunches. Civilization conditions us to rely on our five tangible senses of what we see, hear, feel, smell and taste, and so our intuition may be suppressed.

British industry sectors which rely heavily on reading people and situations and making high level decisions based on a hunch are now following the American trend and are tuning into how to turn the power of the unconscious mind into a potential business tool. Already major banking, insurance and recruitment companies are beginning to send key personnel on courses to learn how to develop their intuition.

Intuitive methods will achieve similar results to other facilitation methods, and during the process people gain confidence in their own ability to use intuition when making decisions and solving problems.

Learning to wait for the right time to act, allowing key factors to emerge and changing course in midstream, are all intuitive activities.

PRACTISE GETTING INTUITIVE

🔊 Before finalizing any decision, ask yourself: 'How do I really feel about this?' Ask colleagues how they feel about what they are about to do. Self-disclosure about your own feelings will help colleagues to loosen up before describing the often taboo subject of feelings when making a business decision.

🔊 Pay close attention to your own first impressions and initial feelings when faced with a new situation. Catch your first impressions and begin to recognize the difference between a gut reaction in the pit of your stomach and feeling the hairs on the back of your neck standing on end. Record the types of events that follow these feelings.

🔊 If you experience strong visual pictures with emotions attached to them, take time and ask yourself what your mind is telling you with this flash of insight. Notice associated tastes, whether they are pleasant or bitter, and heightened smells that may signal victory or defeat. Recall a first impression and ask yourself: 'If this had a smell, what would it be? How would it taste? If I had to make a decision right now, what would it be?'

🅠 Write down your intuitive impressions and keep track of the results. Once you realize how accurate your intuitions are, you will pay more attention to the results.

🅠 Begin team meetings by asking everyone to note briefly their thoughts, feelings or impressions about the meeting's agenda as they occur. Then ask each person to mention something they wrote down on their list.

SUMMARY

🅠 Know what you want and share your dreams with others.

🅠 Optimism is not enough; practise getting good ideas regularly.

🅠 Listen to and trust your intuition.

CHAPTER 3
Being on Purpose

- **What do you feel passionate about?**
- **Could you change things to make your life more purposeful?**
- **In what ways could you make a difference?**

If you die without finding a purpose, you leave the world nothing but a mass of waste product.

MARSILIO FININO,
FIFTEENTH-CENTURY ITALIAN PHILOSOPHER

PURPOSEFUL PEOPLE

Why is it that some people with perhaps only average abilities achieve outstanding successes in life, while others with amazing talents achieve little? The answer is that being 'on purpose' is what counts – if you have a belief in a long-term purpose you really care about and you burn to make it happen, then all your thoughts, actions, achievements and goals will flow together towards realizing your dreams.

Your key to success is to build a strong purpose that you care about with a passion strong enough to take you through the difficult times. The joys of being on purpose are immeasurable. When you are purposeful and constantly motivated towards your target, your senses are heightened and you feel truly alive. Purposeful people feed off the energy surges from remembered past successes to create bigger, bolder and more inspiring challenges to master. Confident that they will succeed, they radiate an energy that is charismatic and others are drawn to their vibrancy and action like moths towards a flame.

Anyone who meets Pete Cohen is immediately struck by his sense of purpose. If you have attended his 'Lighten Up' weight loss programmes, you will also have been struck by the fact that his body is covered in bars of chocolate. Small Picnic and Mars bars are stapled to every square inch of his hat, jacket and clothing.

'Do you like chocolate?' he asks the audience. 'I luuve choc-o-late' he whispers seductively. 'In fact I luuve it so much that I like putting it all over my body. You wanna see some more?' He opens up his waistcoat to reveal even more confectionery stapled to the inside of his clothes. Pete toys with his chocolate bars while making great play of deciding where to put them, and jokes 'I like to choose where I put my chocolate, I might put it around my stomach, or I could move it to my butt.' With the audience transfixed, he delivers the killer punchline: 'Of course, you don't have any choice where you put your chocolate – when it's on the inside of your body.'

And so begins a workshop which records that a staggering 68 per cent of participants not only lose pounds but have maintained their weight loss after one year, compared with 5 per cent for other programmes.

Watching Pete perform, you might think that life has always been easy for him – but you would be wrong. He was marked out from an early age as a low achiever. His teachers said he would never amount to anything and he left school at 16 with no qualifications. Later in life he was found to be severely dyslexic.

Pete is now a professional motivator, he went on to get a good education and has worked as a sports psychologist and coach to some of the most famous athletes in the UK. He set up his own business, started his revolutionary slimming programme and has become a TV personality who motivates millions of viewers to lose weight, conquer their phobias and increase their confidence on several popular self-help programmes. He says: 'I don't take myself too seriously, I'm approachable – and that means I can help people make changes. The secret is to make it easy for them.'

He achieved his aims by turning his teachers' negative predictions about him into a motivational tool that spurred him towards his dreams. He worked hard and now has an impressive list of qualifications in almost every aspect of sports and fitness training as well as coaching and remedial work.

His second motivation was self-belief. He says: 'I knew what I wanted, so I spent plenty of time visualizing my success. I always knew exactly what it would look like and feel like. I knew that however long it took, I would eventually succeed if I kept myself focused on the outcome I wanted. If you lose sight of your goal, it's easy to lose heart when times are tough.'

It took Pete more than ten years of hard work and determination to achieve the success he now enjoys. His top tip?

Motivate yourself – nobody else can do it for you!

THE KEY TO BEING 'ON PURPOSE'

Sum up

- The key to being 'on purpose' is to find what you want to do.
- Then work out how you can serve others by achieving your purpose.
- Then look for a way you can combine the two and make money doing what you love.

Purpose brings energy, focus, new ways of thinking, feeling and looking for ways to achieve your aims in life. Purpose comes from self-knowledge. The Progress now box on page 58 has some idea-sparking questions for you to answer — think about what your answers reveal about your personal aptitudes and passions.

Some people may say that their purpose in life is to make huge amounts of money. However, money is only an exchange mechanism, a lifeless pile of paper to be exchanged for the feelings associated with owning the things you want. When you dig deep you find that much of what people want from wealth is to change the way they 'feel'. Aristotle Onassis, the Greek shipping billionaire, when asked why he still worked so hard when he was so fabulously rich replied 'Because I never want to experience poverty again'. He was rich beyond most people's dreams and yet the fear he felt at the thought of losing all his money and being poor spurred him on to greater effort.

Progress now

What are the things that you are naturally good at and perform with ease? Are you a good communicator, a natural athlete, do people say that you are a clown, or can you pick up on a situation quickly and effortlessly? Are you intuitive or a born organizer, good in a crisis, sympathetic, or a persuasive speaker? The abilities and talents that you excel at are often indicators of where your life purpose lies – especially if you enjoy doing those things.

Have you achieved any successes in relation to your talents? What things do you consider to be your greatest successes? It may be as simple as lending a sympathetic ear to someone in distress or something you did that other people remarked has improved things. You might have an aptitude for making sensible decisions or have won recognition for boosting company sales. Write down how it benefited others and how it made you feel.

Do you have a cause that you feel passionate about? Something that holds your attention because you care deeply about it. Could your life purpose be based around it? Write down your answers – somewhere in there is the key to finding your purposeful direction in life.

Progress now

Imagine a future when you have already achieved your purpose. What feelings do you want to attach to them? Do you want a 'feeling of freedom', 'being loved', 'recognition' a 'feeling of security' or some other kind of feeling? Do your feelings come mostly from having accumulated vast sums of money or are they tied in more closely to your personal achievements?

- Have a purpose.
- Find out how you can serve others by achieving your purpose.
- Devise a way to spread the knowledge.

By focusing on their vision, motivated people create a model in their minds of what success looks like, then their imagination kicks into action to create compelling ideas that propel them towards their goals. This does not mean they will not fail at times, but their happiness does not depend on external circumstances; their purpose is strong enough to carry them through the difficult times.

A solicitor who had worked his way up the ladder to become a senior partner in his firm did not feel either happy or successful. He had a wonderful home and family, whom he adored, and a good lifestyle – yet on most days he said he felt his achievements were empty and that he wanted to do something else. He, like many people, had worked really hard towards a purpose that was not his own, but one his parents had chosen for him.

- Whose purpose are you following?
- Is it time to change what you are doing?
- Did you choose the life you are living now? Or did someone else choose it for you?
- Or did you fail to make a choice and just happen to end up where you are by default?

Self-knowledge lets you understand more about how you think in relation to the world. It is the key to discovering your identity and the types of things you are drawn to. Self-knowledge comes not just from being aware of what is happening around you and in the wider world, but from exploring your own inner space. To 'be on your own purpose', your mind and body must know what you want so that you can develop new behaviours that support your goals.

You will need to develop a level of sensory awareness that most people do not have if you are to hold a strong image of success in your mind, and see possibilities in situations that others cannot see. The ability to see fine details undetected by the casual onlooker is how forensic detectives solve the crime. It is also a tool you can use to see new possibilities in everyday situations.

You already possess tools for noticing very fine details – these are seeing, hearing, feeling, tasting and smelling. Now let's start to fine-tune your sensory acuity.

All of our impressions of the world come from our senses of seeing, hearing, feeling, smelling and tasting. The jury is still out on whether we have a sixth sense called intuition. When a person talks, many of their descriptive words will be in their most dominant sensory system. Thus, someone who is predominately visual might say 'I see what you mean' or 'I get the picture', whereas someone who is auditory might reply 'I hear what you're saying' or 'that rings a bell'. Someone who relies on gut feelings might say: 'I feel we should do this' rather than 'I think we should do this'.

Knowing people's dominant sensory systems allows you to know more about how they take in information from the world outside, and the sorts of things they are likely to notice. You can build rapport with them by switching your language to their style – 'visual' or 'auditory' – so you can begin to understand a little more about how they see the world. If you intend to build your purpose by fulfilling other people's needs, trying on their sensory systems will become essential to you when creating new ideas for products, training programmes or concepts that you hope to interest them in.

Modelling other people's behaviour and noticing the things they do well will form part of the tools that you can use when creating high expectations of yourself, especially when you need to develop new skills and maintain them. Once you are clear on the outcome you want to achieve, and you have found somebody who can already do it, you can model them to find out what their strategy is (see Chapter 8).

Americans Richard Bandler and John Grinder are famed for the work they have done on modelling human excellence. They studied therapists who were judged to be particularly good at treating patients to discover exactly what they did. A good starting point for finding out more is the book *Frogs into Princes* by Bandler and Grinder (Eden Grove Editions, 1990). Their work, which became known as Neuro-Linguistic Programming (NLP), showed that people who had particular skills and behaviours used strategies to achieve them. They found that often, when people are extremely accomplished at a task, their skills are so intuitive that they are unaware of what they do to get good results.

What Bandler and Grinder noticed was that people use strategies for everything they do, from tying their shoelace to driving a car or addressing an audience. Interestingly, it was found that people who did not do things well also ran strategies for the things they could not do. Consequently, all human behaviour, including yours, is based on strategies, which are reproducible. By understanding how your own and other people's strategies work, you can learn to reproduce the ones you want at will. If you want to excel at something you are not yet good at, you can model someone else who possesses the behaviour in order to quickly enhance the skills you need to achieve your aim.

PURPOSE COMES FROM KNOWING

Purpose comes from knowing that the things you do align with your beliefs and values.

🔖 **Values** are things which are important to you – You may value good manners, good service, punctuality or that people tell you the truth. Furthermore, you can usually see whether these values are being upheld.

🔖 **Beliefs** are different from values. You can believe things that are not actually true. You can believe that your house is safe, until it floods or the ceiling falls in. You can believe that you have a happy relationship until your partner tells you they are leaving you. At this point you start to re-examine your beliefs about how safe your house is or how good your relationship was.

Whole groups of people or nations can share the same beliefs. The American nation believed it was invincible until terrorists flew an aircraft into the side of the World Trade Center. At times like this, when a disaster happens, people have the painful task of re-examining what they had believed to be true in order to know what they now believe.

FINDING OUT WHO YOU REALLY ARE

Beliefs, values and purpose are our drivers, they are the things that motivate us and make us who we are. If you do not know what drives you, you cannot motivate yourself to be more effective or press your own triggers to get the results you want from life.

What gets you out of bed and into your place of work in the morning? Is it pain or pleasure? Are you an action person designed to hit the tarmac running? Do you have a mission in mind? Does greeting another work day bring a smile to your face, or a knot to your stomach that tells you you are stressed out, unappreciated or working for a lousy boss? If you are unhappy, your health suffers. Unhappy people make themselves inefficient, sick, absent, and eventually leave their jobs.

In a recent survey of employers, 80 per cent said that their workers suffer stress. Heart attacks are most likely to happen on a Monday morning, either on the way to or on arrival at work.

There are thousands of groups of people keenly interested in finding out what makes you tick. They may be manufacturers who want to sell you their products, newspapers, magazines, fashion designers, TV sports channels or internet providers. Governments want to persuade you that what they are doing is the right thing to influence your voting habits, and many employers use psychometric testing to find out what motivates potential staff.

Companies whose competitive edge rests with its workers need a committed workforce. Yet as organizations downsize, merge and have fewer permanent staff, they can no longer bank on the loyalty of remaining staff, many of whom do not feel secure in their jobs. What can companies offer, besides money, to attract people who are committed to the work they do?

VALUES AT WORK

The answer, says Wendy Sullivan of Discovery Works, an independent workforce trainer, is that 'companies must offer meaningful work in relation to people's lives and values'. She says that 'Often, managers read about values and think they're a good thing to have. So they'll stick them on the walls and think, "We now have a values-led company". Except it doesn't work – people need to have an emotional connection to, and an understanding of, company values. All staff need to be given the opportunity to question, challenge, influence and get involved with company values, so they can develop a deep, shared understanding of them.

'Values, once installed in the workplace, provide the basis for true staff empowerment. If the staff know the values the company is based on, and are aware of the behaviour that springs from holding those values, they are then in a position to make clearer work decisions for themselves.'

Organizations that are not values-led are obliged to have many rules and manuals that give all the 'dos' and 'don'ts' in a very bitty, procedural way, and may also need several layers of management to direct staff.

'From the company's viewpoint it's good news because you don't need huge numbers of procedures in place, or masses of management. To make the most of a values-led company, staff should be given the tools that enable then to understand how their own and the company's values might connect in a way that brings meaning to their life through work. And that's going to help the person feel that they are leading a rewarding life.'

Nevertheless, what happens if, when you get in touch with your own values, they are not compatible with your organization's values? Wendy Sullivan says that 'Some staff may stay put and go through the motions of doing the job. Others may decide to change a couple of values that no longer serve them well and so become more aligned with company values. Some employees may decide to move on – which is an advantage to everyone concerned. It's not useful to the company to have somebody who has totally different values, hanging around and not buying into things. And it's not useful for the individual either, because it's unlikely they are getting any job satisfaction.'

WHAT IS WORK LIKE FOR YOU?

Everyone can find a metaphor for how they would like to think about work, i.e. work is 'like a roller coaster'. This might mean that some bits are safe and boring, and others are fast and out of control. Or work can be 'like gardening' where you are nurturing seedlings and growing plants to be in harmony with each other. Work can be 'like a war', you need weapons and skilled fighters beside you to vanquish enemies.

When you ask people to think of a metaphor for how they would like to feel about work, that metaphor will contain their values.

What is important to you about the work you do?

BEING ON PURPOSE

Nick Williams author of *Unconditional Success* (Bantam Press, 2002), says, 'People often change their jobs for one of two reasons – desperation or inspiration. Often it takes a bit of both to get them to shift. They're motivated to get away from what they don't enjoy, say overwork or unrewarding jobs. But when you say: "What do you want to do then?", they don't know.

'Before deciding to make meaningful changes in your life you first have to identify what is important to you. Ask yourself "What is really important to me in my life, work, relationships – what would I fight for? Where can I start to make changes?"

'Passion is an indicator of what you value, it's what draws you, holds your attention, keeps you thinking about it late at night. It's the one thing you would do if you had all the money and resources in the world you needed – what would you be drawn to then? What work would you do for nothing?'

DECIDE WHAT YOU REALLY WANT, USING VALUES

Start thinking about the things that are important to you and choose a context to work in. You might choose what your values are *in life*, or *in love*, but here we will choose *in work*. Choose six things that you value most about your work. If nothing springs to mind choose from this list and add any more you can think of:

Routine, responsibility, comradeship, advancement, change, high earnings, targets, harmony, helping others, recognition, location, growth, innovation, fame, appreciation, truth, friendly, risk taking, control, respect, loyalty, learning, fun, freedom, precision, confidence, initiative, independence, motivation, socializing, variety, delegation, entrepreneurship, progression route, meaningful, creative, status, working solo, teamwork.

Choose six of these values and beside each one write the reason why it is important to you. It might be:

Creativity is important to me because . . . It lets me express myself. Freedom is important to me because . . . I want to decide what I do.

When you have listed your values, you can number them with the importance you give to each value. If you cannot decide whether you rate one thing over another, write the words on pieces of paper and put them face upwards on the palms of each hand. Look at them and try weighing them up to see which one you decide upon.

As soon as you start thinking about values your brain starts processing the information and the order of some of the things that are important to you may change. Or you may find in a few weeks' time that you have a completely new order to your list of values.

Wendy Sullivan of Discovery Works has an interesting metaphor for the work she has created. She is responsible for generating her own work and says: 'Work — it's like a conveyor belt going past with all these packages wrapped up as presents. And I have to tear the wrappings of as quickly as possible to see what's inside and make sure that nothing gets away.'

It is difficult to set future goals without having a current baseline to compare it with. Before asking yourself the next question, it is important that you already have your metaphor for 'how work is now'.

Metaphors or stories are part of our lives and who we are, we learn lessons from them and are enriched and challenged by them and sometimes, as a result of hearing other people's stories, we change our own.

Progress now

The next question to ask is: 'If my work was just the way I wanted it to be and I were doing the things I wanted to do – what would that be like?'

Describe it in one sentence and take five to ten minutes to get your sentence just right for you.

Your metaphor for what you would like work to be like, once deciphered, may have boiled down to any number of conclusions. It may be:

- I want to work in a successful team and be recognized.
- I want to work alone and be recognized.
- I want to have more control over my working life.
- I want to work less and earn more.

- I want to do something that makes a difference to me and the people around me.
- I want to give my employers more value for their money.
- I want to feel secure and the money from my job gives me that.
- I want more enjoyment from my work as well as earning money.

If by this point you know your purpose in work that's fine. If you don't know then the exercise opposite will help to clarify your purpose.

Stop questioning when you start repeating the same answers because at this stage you probably cannot go any further. A salesman whose metaphor for work was "I want to work in a successful team and be recognised and financially rewarded" answered these questions. He realised that:

- He was already working in one of the most prestigious car sales dealerships in the country.
- He was already working with a successful team.
- He frequently gained recognition and felt good about himself, in fact he was one of the best salesmen on the team.

Progress now

If you have a friend who can ask you these questions, that is great. If not, you will have to ask yourself. Take whatever your metaphor is and put it at the top of a sheet of paper and then ask yourself some questions. Each question is formulated by taking a couple of the descriptive words used in the person's previous sentence and feeding it back to them. For example:

'I want to work in a successful team and be recognized.'

Question: 'And what would that do for you?'

'It would make me **feel good** about myself and give me an adrenalin surge and give me recognition.'

Question: 'And what would **feeling good** about yourself say about you?'

'It would say I am good at what I do, and am working among the best, and **earning the rewards** that come from being the best.'

Question: 'And what would **earning the rewards** say about you?'

'It would say I'd made it on my own merits and am earning the rewards.'

So what was missing? The financial rewards were missing. He worked for a business that set maximum earnings for their salespeople and he was already earning that. He realized a very basic truth, that in order for him to earn a higher salary he would have to leave that job and move into an area such as IT recruitment or insurance sales, where it would be possible to attain really high earnings.

The formula for finding out what you really want to do is:

- Identify what is important to you.
- Clarify what you want.
- Decide which changes to make.

All of this means nothing unless you take follow-up actions. Plant this seed in your mind: 'What steps can I take <u>today</u> to lead me nearer to my goal?'

What is the next action I can take today to make the future I want a reality? It may be small but whatever it is – do it.

DEVELOP YOUR OWN PURPOSE

Remember, the magic formula for being on purpose is:

- 🔖 Find a need that you care deeply about.
- 🔖 Observe what is happening now.
- 🔖 Think about how you could do it differently.
- 🔖 Then fill that need.

Your purpose, beliefs, values and destiny are all intertwined. As your thoughts and actions flow together and your energy for your purpose builds, you will find that opportunities open up for you in often unexpected ways. A chance meeting, a proposal, a snatch of someone's conversation may alert your senses and call you to take actions that propel you towards your goals.

At times like this, when some fast-paced decision making is called for, you may feel like a passenger who has arrived on a station platform as a train is pulling out. For a split second you hesitate because you are unsure of the destination, then there is no more time to think as you hurl yourself on board.

As the doors close and the train speeds away, you realize that things that you strived for are being handed to you now, and events are happening faster than they have ever done before. When serendipity happens, it is best not to labour over how you got your break. Just be joyous that you knew your purpose and trust that this is another link towards your ultimate destination. You paid for your ticket with all the effort and purpose that has brought you to this point.

First believe you can – then start to do it.

SUMMARY

- We all have a purpose in life. If you do not know yours, then find out.
- The images in your mind's eye depict the pattern for your success.
- Begin by aligning your beliefs and values.
- Your actions will then flow towards your goals.

CHAPTER 4
Selling Yourself on Your Goals

- How often do you set timescales and checkpoints to your dreams?
- Do you know how to set your best possible goals?
- Have you learned the 21-day habit to regularly achieve goals?

Saddle your dreams afore you ride 'em.

MARY WEBB, 1881–1927

J.K. Rowling, who wrote the Harry Potter books, ranks amongst the most successful selling authors in the world. This divorced, single mother, living in reduced circumstances, became a multi-millionaire within a short space of time. Her books have already sold 140 million copies and her films are doing well – bringing her an estimated fortune of £226 million within five years.

In an interview, Rowling was asked if she had any difficulty coping with the obvious changes that success had brought her. She replied, 'No', because for five years she had seen the world through the eyes of her main character, Harry Potter, and he was an extremely successful person. Rowling's adjustment to her new lifestyle was not a problem because she had spent years visualizing success. What does this tell you about the benefits of imagining yourself a winner?

Few take the actions

We may daydream about the things we would like to achieve in life, but few people consistently take the necessary actions to propel them towards their goals. It is not that we are lazy or completely unmotivated, in fact in some cases it is simply because we were never taught how to set and achieve goals.

If you have never felt excitement before achieving a long desired goal, then it is difficult to relive previous feelings of exhilaration and pride, and harness them towards making your next experience feel authentic, intense and alive.

Being successful at reaching your goals is the biggest and most exciting gift you can give yourself. To achieve fulfilling goals, you first have to know what you want from life and have the inner awareness of how these things connect to your values and beliefs, and ultimately your life's purpose. Without goal setting there can be no success, so commit your desires to the forefront of your mind to make your purpose a reality.

THE POWER OF SETTING GOALS

While purpose is a long-range target and usually far ahead, goals are shorter. You may have a goal to set up your own business, to run a marathon, get married or increase your learning. Any of these aims might take several years to achieve, but they are all markers along the road to your purpose. You do not stop everything when you get to these goals because they are not your ultimate destination.

How often do you set goals?

- If you feel bored, uninspired or that life lacks sparkle, then check to see when you last set yourself some interesting goals. It could be that you do not set goals and have got into the habit of going along with the ebb and flow of life's events.

- If you do not set your own goals, that does not mean that you do not achieve targets. You may be part of someone else's dreams and purpose, a cog in your employer's production line or your partner's or family's aspirations.

- Do you feel that you do not get the opportunity to have the things you want? Some people lead such an energetic lifestyle, they are too busy doing other things to plan how to achieve the things they want.

◐ If you believe that the breaks that happen for you are luck, then you probably dream and goal set without realizing. Once you begin to consciously plan, guess what happens? You get even luckier.

When you know how to maintain your level of motivation, how you set your goals, and how to follow through with positive actions, you hold the key to success in every area of your life. The art of consciously goal setting is one of the most invaluable mental tools you will ever possess.

Means, motive and opportunity

To set goals and achieve them, you need to employ some of the techniques used by TV detectives. First you need to know whether you have the means, motive and opportunity to reach your goal.

◐ **Means**: Do you have the requirements such as skill, time, money, connections and knowledge that will help you reach your aim?

◐ **Motive**: Do you want your outcome enough to pay the price? Are you prepared not to waver or be distracted from your goal and to follow through to completion?

Opportunity: Do you have the opportunity to go for it, and how much control do you have over the outcome. Although you are unlikely to have complete control over a business or relationship outcome, the more control you have in your power to influence the outcome, the more likely you are to achieve your aim.

Once you have established that all systems are based on the means, motive and opportunity ingredients, it is your beliefs about yourself, and your power and determination to make things happen that will determine how successful you are.

DON'T KILL YOUR DREAMS

Your parents may have set a goal for you as a child, perhaps that you would learn to eat with a knife and fork. They showed you how to do it, praised you for eating nicely and once the habit was established it became easier for you to repeat the process again. Soon, eating with a knife and fork became automatic and you could safely place your food in your mouth without spearing your lips.

Could you imagine what might have happened if the first time you tried it you had decided 'No, I'm not doing this eating with a knife and fork stuff any more – it's much too difficult. I'll just never do it again.' Yet that is precisely the attitude some people take to achieving their goals. They kill their dreams by saying 'I tried that once, it didn't work, I won't bother doing that again.' The fact that you cannot see the means to get something you want does not mean you will not find a way if you puzzle over the situation long enough. All it means is that you have not found the solution yet. Never give up on your meaningful goals, they are your ticket to achieving your purpose in life.

Successful goal-achieving strategies are not just useful for business purposes. They link to every other area of your life, be it

85

financial, career, social, family, mental, physical or spiritual. How we picture ourselves, whether it is as a success or failure, ultimately affects our level of confidence and self-esteem, and our beliefs about the things we are capable of achieving in the future.

Success for many people comes through the career they choose or the talents that they offer in exchange for money and/or recognition. If we really do choose the lives we want to live, then here is an interesting question. Are you, right now, sitting in the location you want to be; doing the work you want to do because it interests or excites you? Are you exchanging your special skills for money and recognition — or are you just doing a job for money?

> Make decisions. Live your life through decisions rather than habits. You will have more control over your life, and enjoy greater success.

PETER THOMSON

You are more likely to reach your goals when they become steps in an overall strategy. For Dela Foster, working in a high class food preparation and delivery service is ideal because it leads into her next goal which is to set up her own restaurant and sandwich delivery service to office workers in the City of London.

SETTING A CAREER GOAL

After university, Dela Foster, 26, worked for a management consultancy. She says: 'I found the first nine months very exciting, but then began to feel disillusioned. Consultancy is an interesting area, but I felt that it doesn't achieve much – its main role is to validate the opinions of the decision maker in a company. If a chairman has to make an uncomfortable decision they'll often get in consultants. You could argue that it's a valid activity to be reassuring people who are making decisions about millions of pounds. But I didn't find it very satisfying. I also felt the job was too desk orientated, I wanted to be actually running the company rather than simply talking about it.'

One evening Dela was pressed for time, she wanted to order a restaurant meal to entertain people at home and couldn't find a company to order from. She says: 'Later I found there was a new business called Deliverance that offered that service – it seemed just like the sort of business I wanted to get involved with.'

Dela's strategy for finding out if joining the company was the right decision was to talk to the owners and do some evening work taking telephone orders to get a feel for the company. She says: 'It fitted the right criteria, it was a young company, a year old with 60 employees and growing. The atmosphere, quality of life and attitude to work at Deliverance felt good, and it was a new and exciting business area to get into.

'I started as assistant manager, looking at new ways to improve the running of the business. I launched another branch of Deliverance the following year in Clerkenwell and I took over the management of it.

'I find the job really exciting: it's exactly what I was looking for in terms of working with people and motivating them and making things run more efficiently. In the 15 months since I joined, the company has doubled its staff to 120 and is still growing. I have total involvement in the business in terms of the people side, the finances, suppliers, customers and planning for the future. In consultancy that's what I longed to do, to be able to see the whole picture and not just have to focus on one element of a business, such as cost cutting.'

Courtesy Cherry Publishing, *Real World Magazine*,
copyright Frances Coombes

What are goals?

- Goals are specific, they are actions you can take that lead in the direction of your purpose.

- Your goals should be personal to you, although they may link into someone else's goals.

- Goals should interest and inspire you.

- Goals are measurable, which allows you to judge how much progress you have made towards reaching your target.

- Goals should be achievable, not so easy that they do not tax you, not so hard that you regularly fail to reach them and so become disillusioned.

- Your goals should be realistic and fit in with who you are and what you are capable of doing.

- Goals should be set within a definite time frame. They should also have definite markers along the route so that you can tell if you are doing well or if you may need to change some of your tactics.

Organizations and businesses often fit many goals within other goals that align to a purpose.

WHEN SETTING YOUR GOAL

- Know what you want and in what context you want to excel.

- Have a plan or route map for getting there.

- Have recognizable markers along the way that will let you know whether you are on target.

- Know that what you are doing does not conflict with other goals you have. It is amazing how easily this can happen. For instance, do you know people who are food conscious and take supplements to improve their health yet still smoke 20 cigarettes a day? Work out a way to stack your goals in the same direction so that they all flow together in the direction of your ultimate purpose.

- Visualize your goal and run action replays so that you will recognize what your achievement will look like when you reach it.

Define your goals

Take a look at your life and ambitions and begin to define your goals. List the headings under which you want to achieve them: 'business', 'work', 'money', 'health', 'relationships'. Under each heading write a list of things you would like to achieve, then include a description that covers how you would like things to change. Do not worry about how you are going to do it at present.

Start with a general statement, such as 'I want to increase my earnings, run my own business, run a marathon, write a bestseller'. Now refine your list and make your ingredients more detailed. If you have said that you want to increase your earnings, get down to the specifics, write down by how much and over what period of time this will happen, and include a target date. Then brainstorm for actions you could take to make it happen.

Align your goals

Now look at your overall list of goals to see if any might align with each other, and if there are any others that are dependent on or could run concurrent with your present aims.

Our goals are not set in isolation, they are usually connected to and involve other people, things, and situations. Constantly ask yourself, 'when I achieve this outcome, what else might it lead to, where else might it take me?'

LEVERAGE IN RELATION TO BUSINESS GOALS

Successful people rarely become that way by accident. Talk to most of them and you will find they had a vision of what they wanted and then made choices about how they would live their lives. By beginning with their outcome in mind, they were able to create a step-by-step plan of the things they needed to do and have in order to make their dreams a reality. An important part of goal setting is to brainstorm until you can find a way to make your ideas or products more desirable to buyers than are your competitors' wares. Goals become really high powered when you discover how to exert leverage.

Goals are more exciting when you set them yourself, choosing things that are important to you and capture your imagination. For instance:

- Think of ten things you would really like to do.
- Imagine yourself doing each one in turn.
- Narrow your choices down to the three which are most feasible.
- Now, don't you want to get started on one of them right now?

When you change a car wheel, the leverage exerted by the jack is what allows you to lift an object 40 times your own weight. In business and sales, leverage (also known as the 80/20 rule) can come from identifying and concentrating on a critical few customers, rather than applying equal energy and attention to all.

To leverage your time when completing a task, remember that 80 per cent of the returns from your daily 'to do' list will come from 20 per cent of the items you have listed, and often from just one item. Avoid falling into the 'busy trap' of racing around completing many small tasks that may be easy or insistent or satisfying, but ultimately achieve little. Instead, focus on the most important task, even though it may not be urgent. Ask yourself: 'Which of these tasks relates directly to my goals?', 'Which will still matter five years from now?'

We asked Peter Thomson how he used his 'to do' list: 'You prioritize tasks – do item one and reprioritize it before you do item two. That way all day long you will be working on the highest priority and if you don't get other stuff done, who cares, because you wouldn't have got it done anyway. Or you'd have been working at the expense of other, more important things.'

At 24, Peter Thomson set up the first of three successful companies and within two years he owned the largest tracing agency in Europe, tracing 4,000 people a month. So how did he achieve his first business success? He says, 'Setting goals is important, I make lists and set goals every single day. But if you are to succeed big time in business you also need a good idea that will give you leverage.'

Thomson says, 'With my first business we offered a new concept on tracing debtors called "risk reversal" which meant we only got paid if we found people. On top of that we charged less than our competitors for the basic tracing service, in order to attract more clients.'

So how could anyone make money from a business like that? He explains, 'I found a formula – if you trace someone once but get paid for it more than once – it's called leverage. So if I traced, say a shopkeeper, I had that information on file. If he owed money to one confectionery business, he probably owed money to others. So I had already done the work once and could sell the results again and again. That's where I made my money.'

Similarly, when Peter decided he wanted to become an audio presenter he used his self-questioning technique. 'I wrote down what I wanted to do – be an audio presenter. The biggest audio presenting company in the world was Nightingale Conant. What got me my foot in the door, because it was different from what anyone else had done, was that rather than going to the company with an idea, I went with a completed product.

'The company was approached by hundreds of people every day saying "I've got this idea for a programme." So I wrote and recorded a programme and took it to them as a completed product. I figured there's no shortage of people in the world with ideas – what's in shorter supply is action. They said, "We love your voice and your material but we're not heavily into the sales market with our audio products." However, I ended up voicing the Nightingale Conant classic "Lead the Field" and have continued with them from there. I've now written hundreds of tapes and audios.

'People say that information is power, but that's a misquote. I meet a lot of clever people who have amassed a lot of information but are not rich, they may even be working for people who are not as clever as them. It's how you leverage information that gives you power in business.'

Courtesy MPMG Ltd, *Sales Director Magazine*,
copyright Frances Coombes

SET YOUR OUTCOMES

Think about something you really burn to achieve, something that is challenging and excites you, but not totally beyond your abilities. From your list of goals, is there one that it is imperative for you to reach now, one that hinges to many other important aims in your life?

Clearly defining your goals is the first step

1. **What do you want?** You may already have some definite goals in mind, but if not then now is the time to get them. From your column headings of perhaps, 'money', 'business', 'work', 'health' or 'relationships', pick something that is important to you in relation to you life's ambitions.

2. **Imagine you already have your outcome**. What will you see, hear, feel and experience that will let you know you have achieved your goal? Athletes practise these sorts of actions every day, imagining they have hit the ball, run the race, lifted the weight and lived the experience many times before the actual event. In this way, they use all of their sensory apparatus to see things they might not otherwise see, play through and correct different actions in their imagination, and feel all the feelings associated with performing brilliantly and

achieving success. When they go onto a pitch, stadium, pool table or boxing ring, they have success hard-wired into their neurology. When it is time to perform, even in teams, they do not have to think about 'Who shall I pass the ball to and will he be there?'; each person's actions are synchronized to achieve the same outcome.

Imagine you have already achieved your outcome
Check for any side effects you have overlooked

1. **Context**. In what circumstances do you want this outcome — business, work, home, social? Are there any circumstances in which you would not want it? For example, your aim might be to acquire better leadership skills so you can take on a more challenging role in your work. But would you want to carry those skills over to dealings with your friends or family? Be aware that a change in thinking style and behaviour in work, if carried into other areas of your life, might change the dynamics of your relationships.

2. **Impact**. How will this outcome affect the people around you? Consider business associates, work colleagues, partner, family, friends. Sometimes relationships break up because one partner is striving to be more successful, while the other stays the same. If your goal will affect your whole family, then involve them and get them to buy into what you are doing at an early stage.

3. **Cost analysis**. What will you gain from having this outcome? What do you get from what you are presently doing? Will you lose anything you value by achieving your outcome? Some business entrepreneurs pay the price of losing their first marriage when they undertake a goal because their beliefs and values evolve whereas their partner's remain the same.

Having the things you need

1. **Control**. How much control do you have over this outcome? You will probably never have complete control, but the more you can influence the outcome, the more likely you are to achieve it.

2. **Resources**. What skills, understanding, information and time do you need to achieve this outcome? Do you have them, or do you know how to get them? Do you need money? Often when you think a situation through you realize that money is only a medium of exchange and that you do not need it. You need what money will buy you – so barter.

3. **Time**. What is a realistic time frame to achieve your goal? Most people work better under deadlines and if you do not set deadlines, your work may expand to fill the spare time you have. Telling others about your plan and announcing the completion date can give you extra motivation to complete if you start to waver.

4. **Obstacles**. What will you do about anything that might get in the way? When dealing with other people or events, bottlenecks and delays are likely to occur. Write a list of what these might be and detail several options you could take to get you past the hurdle. If the delay involves another person agreeing to complete a task by a certain date, and you think they will not meet your deadline ask them at the beginning of the project, 'Can I have your word on that?'

5. **Bridges**. What do this goal and your actions bridge to? Achieving goals opens doors to other possibilities – always be on the lookout for other opportunities.

6. **Going ahead**. What would this outcome say about you as a person? If you achieve this outcome, what else will you get? What is this goal a bridge to? What is the next step to attaining this outcome?

Now do you still want this outcome?

FRAME YOUR PICTURE PLAN

Your goals should fit into an overall strategy. Write them down so that you can refer to them and modify your methods according to any changes in circumstances. Goals that are set in relation to others are more likely to be completed, even when the going gets tough, whereas ones set in isolation are more likely to be abandoned if things do not go to plan.

PERSONAL STOCKTAKING

If you completed the 'weighing up your values' exercise in Chapter 3, you already know the qualities which are most important to you. How do your values fit in with your goals towards your big picture plan? If you value 'freedom', but your goal is to get another job which pays more money, are you really furthering your long-term aims? More money may allow you to take longer holidays in more exotic locations and help you forget about your job. However, unless you can tie in other values you hold about the work you do, will it really make you feel fulfilled or purposeful?

🔃 Think about the successes you have had to date. Which of your attributes have helped you to achieve the things you have done so far?

🔃 What are your biggest assets in your personal 'style'? Are you an ideas and vision person? Are you determined, energetic, enthusiastic? Do you have an ability to see the 'big picture' or overall strategy – something that all business leaders should have? Are you able to home in on small details? Do you have excellent communication and interpersonal skills?

Are there any aspects of your personal 'style' that have let you down in the past? You may have got the ideas but you need some training to develop the skills to convince other people how wonderful your ideas really are.

Strike a balance between seeing what you want, knowing what you have, and acknowledging the training and skills you will need to reach your goals.

Keep things simple to start with and do not over-plan. It is possible to become overwhelmed with the details of how to achieve your goals and to end up feeling disconnected from your final outcome.

Initially practise simple goals over short timescales. Break them down until you reach an action you can take immediately, which will give you plenty of small successes from the outset. If you imagine having achieved your goal and then think backwards in time, you can work out the progressional steps you took to get there. From this action, you can work out whether you have the resources necessary to start your plan moving and what next step to take towards your goal.

TIPS FOR GOAL SETTING

- **Break your goals down into small chunks**. A complete project, such as breaking into and saturating a sales market, or being slim, supple and active, or earning a million pounds may seem daunting. Break your goal down and be determined to take some small steps towards achieving your goal each day.

- **Focus on the progress you are making each day**. To write this book and fit it into an already full schedule, I kept a time log diary with a page for each day I worked on the project. From noticing what worked and what did not, I decided that I would fit at least five 20 minute segments of time to inputting on computer in the early morning when I was at my most productive. I also logged each day how easy or difficult I found the progress. Whenever I reached sticking points, I was able to look back and remember what I was thinking, doing and feeling when I had been working well and found the going enjoyable.

- **Think about your goal constantly**. See yourself achieving it and run action movies in your mind. Use all your senses of seeing, hearing, feeling, taste and smell to associate with your picture more fully. See your movie from different angles in order to view any problems from another perspective.

- 🖎 **Commit your goals to writing**. Keep them simple and use categorical words. 'I want to be thinner' is not a goal, it is a wish. 'I want to be 2 kilos thinner in three weeks' gives you a time frame and target. Write down the specific markers you will see, hear and feel, such as 'I will feel fitter and look fabulous in a new outfit', that will let you know that you have reached your aim.

- 🖎 **Goals should be time-specific**. You may have an overall goal, perhaps over ten years. Break it down into yearly segments and have monthly check-ups to see how you are doing. Have regular weekly planning sessions, say on Friday afternoons, where you build your lists for the following week and work on daily improvements.

- 🖎 **Dealing with obstacles**. When you encounter obstacles to your goals, imagine how people who have already achieved a similar outcome would do it. Take three of these successful people and ask yourself how they would approach this task. Take your time and wait for the answers to come.

- 🖎 **Work smarter – not harder**. Often it is necessary to work extremely hard to get a project started. But if this means you are constantly working under pressure, working long hours, and lacking sleep, your standard of work and ability to think strategically will suffer. Do not get so tied up in your project that you do not have time for anything else. You know where you are headed, so be good to yourself along the way. Take some time to smell the roses and give yourself some enjoyment, and lots of little rewards.

- **Catch yourself doing things well**. Keep a daily events diary of your progress, listing your highs and lows. Especially look for clues to see what triggered changes in your motivation levels, particularly the ones that took you from 'can't do' to 'yes, I'm doing it'. When you know how these states were created, you can create them intentionally.

- **Do a look-back exercise**. At the end of every project, do a look-back exercise and review, and write down what worked well and what did not work. Look at ways of getting better and smoother at what you do, and of improving your efficiency.

- **Review your goals regularly**. Besides asking 'Am I on target?' also ask yourself 'Do I still want this outcome?' Are you still whole-heartedly committed to the initial goals you set, or have new possibilities arisen that might take you on another course? People who do not do regular goals reviews can end up reaching their target and then finding out it was not what they wanted after all.

Get into the habit of setting goals and achieving them

Start with small goals and practise aiming for them with the same level of determination you will carry through to your larger projects. In the beginning look for easy goals so that you can hone your techniques and see yourself as a winner. The more frequently you experience success, the easier it is to expect that you will get the things you want from life and the more likely you are to get them.

21 DAYS TO SUCCESSFUL GOAL SETTING

Practise by changing a personal habit

If you intend to change events in the outside world, a good way to check that your goal-setting techniques are working well is to set yourself an inner space goal on a personal level: one that involves either changing a habit, for instance, slimming, getting fit, giving up something, or learning to do something new, or making a change.

105

Your motivation level is likely to drop when you set goals over a long period of time: 'I want to be thin in six months' time – but this chocolate bar is right beside me now'; 'I want to run a mini-marathon next summer, but I can't seem to get out of bed right now'. Much of your initial enthusiasm may disappear if you think so far ahead. For many people, 21 days is the length of time it takes to install a new habit, so plan your goal in clearly defined chunks to be achieved over three weeks.

- Select a goal to work on for 21 days. It must be something that you really want to achieve and are prepared to give your attention to for this length of time.

- Take one chunk of your goal that you know can be accomplished in three weeks' time. For example, if your goal is to lose 2 kilos in 21 days, break it down into daily tasks. Initially you might read some advice on nutrition, and work out where and at what times of day your trigger points for eating chocolate cake kick in. Over the first few days you might decide you will spend an extra 20 minutes each morning planning your day ahead and preparing your own lunches so you are less likely to go off course.

As you approach your first hurdle, say the afternoon coffee slot when you suddenly get a craving for chocolate cake, you may decide to come armed for this occasion by substituting a tasty nutritional snack. Once your new habit is securely in place, and your craving for chocolate cake subsides, you might decide to stop your morning journey short on alternative days so you can walk an extra 20 minutes and think about what is working in your new regime. Looking back over the previous days to see what worked and what did not you might now decide how to plan your evening meals when you are satisfied your new habit has been installed.

Avoid all or nothing thinking. If you begin to encounter obstacles, say your goal is slimming and one day you long to eat chocolate cake, do not assume that because you did not achieve that day's target your whole project is a failure: it is not. Be kind to yourself and allow for two 'relaxation days' when you can relax your new habit.

If you are not an avid plan setter, put large red dots on your calendar beside each allotted day. Write down what you hope to achieve at the beginning, and on target days write in what you hope to have achieved by that day.

Plan your rewards in advance and treat yourself at the end of every five-day period, or whenever you are likely to go astray if you are not pampered in some way. Seeing your goal written in the date box of your calendar in advance will keep you on course. If you promise yourself something special for staying on target, then do it, otherwise you might have a relapse.

Once you have achieved your 21-day systematic approach to goal setting, check over the next few days to ensure that your new habit has become part of your routine.

SUMMARY

Goal setting and making lists are a top priority.

Keep it simple, and break your goals down.

Check your progress by having markers along your route.

Get into the goal-setting habit, make it as natural as cleaning your teeth.

CHAPTER 5
Challenging Limiting Beliefs

🜋 Do you know how to overcome limiting beliefs that may hold you back from success?

🜋 If you want control over your outcome, have you learned how to manage your state?

🜋 Are you using different perceptual positions to help you gather additional vital information on situations?

The real art of discovery consists not in finding new lands but in seeing with new eyes.

MARCEL PROUST (109)

TIM SMIT'S VISION

Tim Smit's vision created a garden called Eden. On a wasteland site he has created one of the most powerful architectural wonders of our time. With the help, energy and enthusiasm of those around him, he turned his dream into one of the most marvelled at wonders of the world. Tim admits he was a dreamer when he conceived his idea for restoring the Lost Gardens of Heligan in Cornwall, England. Yet his dream has become a reality, which over 1 million people from around the world have come to visit.

He says, 'In restoring the Lost Gardens of Heligan, I began to understand the process by which ideas are turned into action.' His own motto is, 'If you're not on the edge, you're taking up too much space.'

The interesting thing about Smit is his total belief that the right people and situations would turn up at the right time. He also firmly believed that he could be the lynchpin that would be instrumental in building Eden. Yet, if he had written a CV asking to be the architect of such an audacious plan, coming from a musical background, Smit would probably have been turned down because he did not fit the 'criteria' for the job.

Few people extend themselves

Often people don't extend themselves enough to 'live on the edge' and find out what else they might be capable of doing outside their regular sphere of work. How many other potential Smits are there out there, serving customers, selling products, making their money in ordinary jobs?

If you want to succeed in life, you have to create your own dream, with you in the starring role. You have to believe in yourself and expect good things to happen. Project a picture of yourself out into the world as a winner; see it, feel it, anticipate it, until you can almost touch it. Then expect to have good things projected back at you. None of us know what we are capable of achieving. It is only when we step to the edges of our boundaries and beyond, that we begin to discover our true potential.

In this chapter we will teach you how to identify and deal with the limiting beliefs that may stop you reaching your potential goals. The aim is to let you try some techniques for countering self-doubt, so that you can see that these work in the real world. Ultimately, however, you need to take personal responsibility for trying out, practising and incorporating the ideas that work best for you in your everyday life.

GETTING RID OF LIMITING BELIEFS

Have you ever talked with friends about the things you'd really like to do in your life? Only to realize later that you haven't got what it takes to do the interesting or brave thing.

TIM SMIT

Once you have positively established the means, motive and opportunity ingredients described under goal setting in Chapter 4, it is your beliefs about yourself, your abilities and your motivation that will determine how successful you are. Your mission in this chapter, should you choose to accept it, is to bombard your brain with as much evidence as possible that you are a truly competent, confident and capable individual that is priming itself like a heat-seeking guided missile aimed towards its goals.

Of all the things a person can say to themselves when faced with a difficult situation, 'I can't' is potentially the most limiting of all. When you hear someone utter these words, you know that person is boxed in or stuck in a way that is currently cutting them off from finding a solution to their problem.

- I can't do it.
- I can't get through.
- I can't see a way around it.

If you believe you have a problem, then you have one – whether it is real or not. If you watch the actions of someone telling you that they cannot do it, often they will stretch their hands in front of them in a helpless gesture. They are in a state of confusion and are not thinking resourcefully. When someone else offers them a solution to their problem and they are in an 'I can't' frame of mind, they are often likely to dismiss sound ideas as unworkable or turn them down because they simply do not believe that anything will work.

Once we are in a calmer and more resourceful state and we have found a solution, we inform people that we have 'got over it', 'found a way round it', or better still have 'sorted it out'. And 'sorting it out', like a computer data sort, is often what we do; we sift the available information and look for recognizable patterns. We ask ourselves 'Has this problem occurred before?', 'How was it tackled?', and 'What was the outcome?' If we hold a state of curiosity long enough we begin to come up with new patterns for solving the problems.

CHALLENGING HABITUAL THINKING

If you have ever wondered how a newspaper horoscope can fit your circumstances and every other 'Leo's' or 'Scorpio's', it is because it uses a technique similar to hypnotist Milton H. Erickson's model of artfully vague language. The horoscope writer uses vague language and the reader interprets and mentally fills in the blanks according to whatever they feel fits their circumstances. The information is accurate for that reader because they have filtered the incoming information by listening for what they want to hear and put their own interpretation on it.

When we think and speak often we **delete**, **distort** and **generalise** the information we give to ourselves and others according to how we see and feel about ourselves and others and what we think is going on in the world. If we feel bad about ourselves we may treat ourselves harshly, so that when someone pays us a compliment, instead of being pleased, we may be thinking: 'What do they want from me?'

If you questioned your habitual ways of thinking, how many of the everyday statements you make to yourself about situations would stand up to deeper scrutiny? Below are a few common patterns of statements you may hear from others or think yourself, with questions beside them to ask yourself in order to generate more information.

People delete, distort and generalize incoming information.

Deletions	**Questions to get more information**
'I'm not happy with this.'	*What* are you not happy about?
	In what way are you not happy?
'Nobody listens to what I'm saying.'	*Not one single person!*
	Who, specifically doesn't listen?

Cause and effect

'She makes me very angry.'	*How* does she make you angry?
	Has there ever been a time when she didn't make you angry?

Distortions

'All he does is criticize.'	*Always?* Without exception?
'She doesn't want me in her team.'	How do you know that?
'They think I'm useless.'	*How do you know* they think that?

If you find yourself thinking 'I can't do it!' ask yourself the question 'According to whom?', 'What stops you?'

HOW TO CONFRONT NEGATIVE BELIEFS

Progress now

Greg Levoy, journalist and motivational speaker, uses this wonderful written exercise for overcoming limiting beliefs on his 'Callings – Heart at Work' workshops. Take a negative belief that you hold, say 'I can't write a best-seller', 'I can't set up my own business' 'I can't be the most successful salesperson on the planet', and start questioning yourself about why not. Look upon it as engaging in a conversation, or a dual between the negative and positive sides of your brain.

Allow Positive and Negative one line for each statement. Start with a negative statement and, whatever it is, start the next line with a positive one. Each negative statement should comprise why you cannot do something and the following positive statement challenges the assumption.

Example: 'I want to write a best-seller'

Negative: You can't write a best-seller.
Positive: How do you know that?

Negative:	Well, you've never written one before.
Positive:	That doesn't mean I couldn't.
Negative:	Yes it does, you haven't got the discipline.
Positive:	I have got discipline in other things, I could organize better.
Negative:	You haven't got the talent, or the desire.
Positive:	Yes I have, and I've always wanted to write a book.
Negative:	When there's time, but you never have enough time.
Positive:	I could make time . . .

Keep this going and do not stop until one side, either Positive or Negative, is exhausted and gives up because they have no more answers. Of over 80 people at Greg Levoy's workshop who did this exercise, most were surprised that they successfully beat their negative 'I can'ts' into submission. We are often afraid to argue with our negative beliefs, because we are afraid of being proven wrong.

Experiment with this exercise a few times and see what sort of result you get. You may be pleasantly surprised. Another benefit of listing your negative and positive thoughts about a subject is that you can spot whether your thinking becomes distorted.

When you can see where your train of thoughts became derailed, you can take action to begin questioning your negative beliefs and get your thinking back on track. Most people would not let another person constantly put them down without any substantiating facts. Why should your brain be allowed to make negative statements about you without being challenged to support its facts?

Progress now

Think of a time when you may need to influence others. It may be to put your ideas across, to give presentations, talk to colleagues, ask for a favour or for something which you might not necessarily get, for instance a contract.

🔂 Think of an activity that you enjoy doing, which makes you feel confident and you are really good at. As you run your mental movie and associate into the images and become part of them you feel your emotions intensify and become stronger. Notice how, as the colours in the pictures become bigger, brighter, bolder and closer, you just sigh and let all the good feelings wash over you.

🔂 Now shake that image off and put it to one side for a moment. Just think about how giving your presentation or influencing task will be easier once you bring across your confident and happy relaxed feelings from your more empowered state.

🔂 As you see yourself watching an internal movie of you giving your talk or presentation, notice that you have distanced yourself and are not in the picture – you are actually watching the movie from outside. You can observe in a more detached way what is happening from this back-row position.

Associate back into the activity you enjoy by running your feel-good movie again to the point where you feel most powerful, confident and alive. As your feelings become stronger, touch your thumb and forefinger together as an emotional trigger and feel yourself leap, taking those strong, positive emotions into your your second picture where you want to experience a successful outcome. You are no longer watching a drab or uncomfortable movie, you are actually in it. But you have brought all the strength, determination and confidence with you from your most empowering feelings and images.

Remember the strong feelings you had when you pressed your thumb and forefinger together at the height of your emotional intensity when you changed your mental movie? You can use that action as an anchor associated with your good feelings in the future. With a little practice, you will be able to recall and trigger this powerful emotional state just by pressing your thumb and forefinger together and bringing your empowering feelings into your next visualization.

We naturally change states

A person may work at a supermarket checkout counter, where they behave in a restrained and predictable way. Yet on Saturday night everything changes, they dress up and look fantastic. Before leaving home they engage in rituals to pamper themselves, smell good, feel sexy and great, and run images of themselves being the greatest dancer on the floor. Guess what happens? They go out, enjoy themselves, get noticed, they get talked to and chatted up. What happens then on Monday morning back at the checkout? Do they become invisible? No, they change their state to perform a task in a way appropriate to their job situation.

What would happen if they decided that for just 20 minutes every morning they would go into disco chat up and energy mode as they served customers? They might get the sack, they might get noticed, they might get promoted, they might get customers enquiring about how they are. They might also start to become more flexible in their behaviour and realize that they can choose how they feel and act. We all have a choice about how we feel and act in any situation, we do not always have to go with the automatic response of the crowd.

Our feelings are the most important things we possess. They dictate whether we feel happy, sad, unloved or hurt, welcome or outcast. We may think that other people influence them, but actually we can choose to manage our internal state and how we choose to feel. How often have you heard someone say, 'She makes me angry'? The truth is they do not make you angry, you allow yourself to feel angry about whatever that person said. By allowing your state or how you feel to be dictated by another person, you are giving up your power to someone else who can decide at a whim how they will 'make you' feel.

As many as one-third of the populations of some countries indulge in drug taking mainly because it changes the way they feel about themselves, how vividly and differently they see the world, and how happy, successful and loved they feel – for a short time only. Many crimes committed are drug-related, and some addicts are prepared to swap their self-esteem, families, liberty and eventually their lives for tablets or a powder that lets them chase their 'feeling good' state.

CHOOSE YOUR PATTERNS FOR SUCCESS

How you choose to feel and the state you choose to operate in can be within your control. That is not to say it will be like getting high on drugs; it will not be so ruinous. We all repeat patterns for the things we do, even that which we are repeatedly unsuccessful at.

Switching states, that is creating an association between two experiences to actively create a strong mental state, is used by many sports- and businesspeople, public speakers and musicians, and others who need to give consistently excellent performances at peak state.

Most people can recall and associate a sad experience with sad or bad feelings at will. All it takes to trigger their mental movie is to say to them 'Remember when . . .', and they do the rest themselves. Their eyes will fix on a spot where they see the events happening, their shoulders will crumple, their breathing will slow down as they relive the emotions they felt that first time. So, why not choose a ritual that is linked to success? Use it as a trigger to recall a time when you felt truly alive and powerful, when everything you did was magic.

(123)

Losers visualise the penalties of failure. Winners visualise the rewards of success.

DR ROB GILBERT

To get used to anchoring good feelings, pick a personal moment of success that you have experienced, and vividly run through the events several times in your mind until you can recall it with ease. Then take the associated feelings and memories attached to it, and save them in your best memories store, like freeze framing a mental and sensory snapshot. When the experience is at its highest point, use a signal, such as pressing your middle finger and thumb together, to recall the good emotional state. In the future, by repeating the finger press action, you will be able to play your success movie at any time you need to feel powerful, successful and in control.

THINKING PITFALLS TO AVOID

🚫 **Avoid all or nothing thinking**. Sometimes, when we work hard to reach a goal, things do not always go to plan. It is easy to slip into the 'all or nothing' kind of thinking. However, if given free rein, negative thinking can fire a chain of negative thoughts designed to sabotage your efforts, and stop you breaking through your next boundary to success. If you catch yourself slipping into the 'I can't do this', 'I'll never finish' and 'Why did I think I could do it?' vein of thought, which is designed to paralyse you with anxiety and make you less effective – change your thinking immediately.

🚫 **New projects can take much initial effort** and may be compared to a jet taking off. The plane uses its maximum capacity of fuel to convert into the energy it needs to take off from the ground and to become airborne. Once in flight, it cruises using only 37 per cent of the fuel it required for take-off.

🚫 **If part of your plan does not work, keep your outcome in mind and try something different**. Often what happens when we make plans and set targets is that we may have to change them a little, but we still end up at the right destination.

CHANGE VIEW POINTS

If you are running negative thinking loops, you might be too close to the situation you are dealing with to have a rational perspective about what is going on. At times like this, it is often good to stand back and distance yourself from the situation for a while, maybe going off somewhere and having a cup of tea can help to put the situation into perspective.

> Before you can know how another man thinks you must walk a mile in his moccasins.
>
> NATIVE AMERICAN SAYING

We adopt different perceptual positions constantly. Sometimes we get involved and are close up and personal, and we feel strong emotions about what is happening. At other times we can distance ourselves from events and this helps us to think more objectively. Each type of observation gives us different types of information about the subject.

If you have not found a solution to your problem using other means, then try adopting different viewpoints and asking yourself questions about the situation. This will give you more valuable information about the situation than you can gain by observing it from only one point of view.

126

PUTTING IT ALL TOGETHER

There is a saying that if the only tool you have is a hammer, then the solution to every problem will be a nail. Now that you have amassed a powerful toolkit that you can use for problem solving and overcoming limiting beliefs weigh up each technique and think about how useful it might be, and in what kinds of circumstances. When you execute a problem-solving technique, notice what changes, how it changes, and whether the result you get is the one you wanted. You have the power to take personal responsibility for motivating yourself and others to make things happen – use it.

SUMMARY

- Beliefs are your most important tool. The strength of your belief in a plan is what determines whether you will carry it through.

- Changing your language also changes your thoughts and actions.

- Use precise questioning as a tool to gather information and confront negative beliefs.

- Do not allow your brain to make negative comments about you, without challenging it to support facts.

- If you want control over your outcome, learn how to manage your state.

- Using different perceptual positions can help you to gather additional information on situations.

CHAPTER 6

Creating the Circumstances for Success

- Do you already know which additional skills and abilities you need to acquire to move towards your goals?

- When did you last seek out new techniques to improve your influencing skills?

- Are you moving in the right circles for success?

Man's mind, once stretched by a new idea, never regains its original dimensions.

OLIVER WENDELL HOLMES JR

Your motivation does not have to stop when you close this book. In fact, for many people, books are a starter point that whets the appetite for more knowledge, and marks the beginning of their journey towards mastery of a subject and a more successful self.

There are thousands of different types of motivational talks, seminars and workshops to choose from; the trick is to find one that is right for you. This chapter gives you an overview of two completely different types of motivational trainings. The first is extreme and physical, designed for personal development and to enable people to move through limiting belief barriers that might be holding them back. The second training uses a combined networking and training approach, and is aimed at ambitious salespeople who are seriously committed to increasing their wealth. The resulting 100K Club is founded on the belief that ambitious birds of a feather should flock together for support and encouragement, and then get all the training they need to lead them to success.

> Always listen to experts. They'll tell you what can't be done and why. Then do it.
>
> ROBERT HEINLEIN

WALKING ON FIRE

Teambuilding is a dangerous pursuit these days. Not content with sit-down training sessions and role playing, staff take to white-water rafting, paintballing and abseiling in an attempt to aid office communication.

Firewalking is just one of the fashionable, if risky, pursuits undertaken by teams looking for inspiration in the name of motivation. But what is the idea behind it and is it relevant to life in the workplace and beyond?

The firewalk

Firewalk leader Simon Treselyan of Starfire training explains: 'The idea of firewalking is very emotive, so people have to overcome the illogical fears they have before they can walk across coals. The firewalk provides a controlled environment where people can make a dramatic change in their lives by moving from "can't do" to having achieved something which they thought was impossible within an incredibly short timespan. Once they've done it they realize they can take that energy and way of thinking and use it to transform other areas of their life, so they can translate the process directly to whatever they want to change.'

As the flames leap higher, it is a reminder that people have been burned in firewalks. The dangers were highlighted in 1998 when seven insurance salesmen from Eagle Star needed hospital treatment, two of them at a special burns unit, after attempting a firewalk at the end of a motivational training day. In that instance, hot coals were put into a metal tray which produced extreme heat, like a barbecue. Could that happen at Starfire? 'No,' says Treselyan, who only uses wood, with no base or tray. 'Wood is a poor conductor of heat and so long as one walks quickly and is not in contact with the surface for very long, there is not enough time for skin to burn.'

The psyching up before the walk also helps to suppress any pain, according to John Humberston, Professor of Physics at University College London. It helps people get into a 'mind over matter' state when they take the first step beyond their natural boundaries.

Simon, an ex-army special forces interrogator, coordinator and operator says, 'Basically the stuff I teach people now has been learned in extreme circumstances. I've moved on from the more negative parts, the aggression, the almost not caring how you do things to get results. I have looked at human behaviour, both positive and negative, and ways to be able to influence that behaviour to inspire people to take on new learnings and go beyond their perceived barriers.'

Is the training a little like tribal initiation? Simon states that 'Some of it has been taken from the rites of passage of many civilizations throughout history. The firewalk has been used by native Americans and Hawaiians as an initiatory rite. Passing through the fire moves them through a portal into manhood. Breaking an arrow by walking forward against an obstacle with the metal tip against the soft part of the throat, which we did earlier, is taken from the Fijian ritual of bringing women into maturity – so yes, it's tribal. These rituals have been used by mankind for thousands of years and have an historical validity and real meaning for human beings.'

When asked if the training appeals to women as much as it does to men, Simon replies: 'Although there is a lot of what could be construed as macho-testosterone stuff, it actually brings out more sensitivity in males and more focus in females. Fifty-five per cent of the people on our trainings are women, so they out-

number the men. Women want what the men have always had —
career structure, focus, and the ability to make money and
determine their own future. And this is a very powerful
mechanism to make sure that they can have that.'

What are the core issues that people have to deal with before
they will walk across hot coals? 'I believe that the greatest
instinct of human beings is not survival but to do that which is
familiar — like staying in a job or relationship when you know you
should get out. Basically people here are learning how to get
from one place to another by moving themselves through
difficult circumstances.

'When we do things that are unfamiliar we feel stressed, fearful,
all of the things which stop us sometimes from moving on.
People stay in destructive relationships or unrewarding jobs
because they don't know how to do anything else. We even have
a saying, "Better the devil you know". People will trot out lots of
reasons to explain why they're staying where they are. The truth
is that usually they're just too frightened to move on.

'What the firewalk does very effectively is provide a controlled
environment where they can make a dramatic change in their
life by moving from "can't do" to having achieved something

which they thought was impossible within a few seconds. Once they realize that they have overcome one incredible fear through the power of their own positive thinking then they often start to change other things in their lives that might be holding them back from achieving their full potential.

'Having done it they realize they can take that energy and way of thinking and use it to transform other areas of their life, so they can translate it directly to whatever else they want to change.'

Motivation, mental focus and mind storming, goal setting and planning are the core of some of Treselyan's courses. But, in eight hours, can he really take someone who is bored, lacks discipline or has an aversion to structuring or planning ahead, and turn him or her into a motivated, goal-setting individual? Treselyan says: 'Yes, you can do it in an hour if you use the right tools. If you use boring mediocre tools then you're not going to make someone highly motivated and highly productive. But a firewalk is very emotive. It gets people's whole attention — not just on the walk but on every detail of the planning. People's emotions are engaged, they take charge of their personal state management, their energy levels and the goal-setting techniques around performing a firewalk.

An exhilarated bunch of tired but happy firewalkers have finally made their walks to rousing applause. They whoop and run about stopping occasionally to hug, swap stories, examine feet, and gaze at each other through team-bonded tears.

But once the firewalk is over and the feet are being nursed, how useful is the exercise seen in relation to work life? For the Guardian team, there were mixed reactions. Views ranged from one person who didn't do the walk and saw it as a pointless, painful task, to others who saw it as a life-changing experience.

Isn't firewalking dangerous? Don't some people still get burned? 'Not usually,' says Treselyan, 'but people have to overcome the illogical fear they have about firewalking. They think: "Oh my god I'm going to get burned". Yet many of them are quite happy to do something like abseiling which has a proven track record of killing people. No one has died in firewalking, and the most that could happen is that you'll get a slight blister, which is the same kind of blister you'll get wearing ill-fitting shoes.'

All 20 people who did the walk said it was a brilliant experience. Simon says, 'Yes, I'm pleased about that. But I'm absolutely delighted that ten of those people also said it was a life-changing experience that made them feel capable of achieving much more.'

Why does Simon Treselyan choose such dangerous pursuits such as the arrow to the throat ritual, walking on glass and firewalking to move people on? 'I have an unshakeable belief and passion that every person deserves as a human right to be the best that they can be, to raise themselves to their fullest potential and to be absolutely fulfilled. I am passionate about self-fulfilment and will strive to bring that idea to as many people as want to listen to me. I recognize that some people don't want this, they are quite happy to be mediocre and second-rate because it means that they are never going to be challenged. They're always going to have an excuse for not succeeding. But for those people, who actually want to see what they're made of, to be the best that they can be, then I will work with them and make them the best.'

(Courtesy of Reed Business Information Ltd, *Personnel Today Magazine*. Copyright Frances Coombes)

THE 100K CLUB FOR TOP PERFORMERS – WHERE PERFORMANCE COUNTS

The 100K Club is a forum for salespeople who are determined to be the best at what they do. Its founder Alex McMillan, author of *Q Learning: Entrepreneur* (Hodder Headline, 2003), believes that attending training courses alone rarely produces lasting behavioural changes.

He says: 'To master sales you need to feel confident you already have the skills to solve problems, create options and have influence over resulting outcomes. To do this best, people need to see the big picture, to network and to spend time away from work colleagues but in the company of other ambitious salespeople.'

The 100K Club is designed specifically for people who want to excel. McMillan says: 'Here they can distance themselves from work and colleagues and discuss whatever's on their mind. It may be current selling strategies and how to improve them, or how to tackle any obstacles that are blocking them from achieving peak performance right now.'

One session – 'It's not over until I win' – explores how to keep going through setbacks and disappointments by looking at the thinking styles of self-made millionaires and billionaires such as

Richard Branson, Bill Gates, Aristotle Onassis and Ray Kroc (McDonald's). As an exercise, participants compare their own mind-sets with that of the millionaires and look for any conflicting beliefs they hold which might seriously inhibit achieving outstanding financial success.

What is the first thing a salesperson would have to do to ensure they earn 100K? McMillan says that rule number one is to be employed by a company where it is possible to earn £100K. He says, 'I was coaching someone who was a top sales performer working for a prestigious car company and he was on top earnings of £35,000. I said: "You cannot make £100,000 a year by staying there." So his next move has to be to get out into whatever sales area he has the potential to earn 100K in at the moment, it could be IT recruitment, financial services, whatever.

'Another simple but effective thing to remember is that people who earn over 100K always take control when they go anywhere and go with an outcome in mind. A sales lead, a tip and ideas, whatever – they don't leave without them.'

McMillan believes that often insecurity drives salespeople – not the promise of the Porsche. He says, 'They're not moving towards the bonuses, they're moving away from the fear of not selling enough.

'A lot of incentives for salespeople are aimed towards some form of pleasure, "If you hit the target you get a bonus or a holiday". But in practice it's often the away from strategies that are the most powerful, "If you don't hit the targets we'll fire you all". Obviously, sales managers don't really want to do that. But there are ways to do it which are used by good management.

'When I was selling, if you were in the bottom half of sales nobody gave you any pressure, but managers wouldn't spend time with you, they'd always talk to their top performers, so you wouldn't be in the inner circle – you wouldn't go to lunches with them. The people who were cut out of the inner circle were often motivated to hit their targets because they wanted to move away from that feeling of rejection. Those low performers may have felt bad but it's unlikely that they were consciously aware of the away from pain strategy that was motivating them to perform.'

The workshop 'Managing those magic moments' asks what gets you into your peak performance state. McMillan says that 'Even top salespeoples' performances go up and down, it's just the best have learned to have less of a dip than others and to get back on target more quickly.

What do top performers do to bring themselves back on target quickly? McMillan claims that 'The beliefs people hold about themselves affect whether they achieve their aims or not. So a large part of getting back on form is to ask yourself lots of questions and then leave your channels of communication to yourself open so you hear the answers.

'These people have already got all the tools they need to do that job at the top level, and while they're in the trough, something is stopping them performing. They don't need training: they need access to what they've already got. Quite often their problems are emotional ones and we use a whole range of techniques that are brilliant for sorting these things out. For instance there are some very simple questions people can ask themselves such as "What would I need to do to get me back on track?" "What's the next action I can take towards it?"

'Our state of mind is geared by the questions we ask ourselves, more than the ones from people around us. We don't do it consciously, but if something went pear-shaped people start to think "What went wrong?", "What did I do?", and the brain gives answers to those questions that may undermine people so that they go into a negative spiral.

INTERVIEW

'Positive thinking is essential – so rather than letting your brain randomly choose the questions and answers it gives you, start to choose them yourself. Work out half a dozen positive questions, put them on the wall and wake up each day and go through them. For example, on my office wall I've got: "What are the six things that I am really happy about right now?" Next question is "What reward am I going to give myself in the future?" – I go through that every morning, it's simple, doesn't take more than 30 seconds but it gets me thinking positively.'

Courtesy of Quest Media, *Selling Financial Services*,
the magazine of the Association of Independent Financial Advisers.
Copyright Frances Coombes

SUMMARY

🐾 Feeling comfortable does not always get you ahead; you sometimes need to take risks that take you away from your comfort zone and push you beyond your current boundaries.

🐾 Plan every detail of your new task, engage your emotions and take charge of managing your personal state, energy levels and goal-setting techniques.

🐾 To be successful you need to see the big picture, to network and to spend time away from work colleagues but in the company of other ambitious people.

CHAPTER 7
Thinking Styles

- Do you know how your own internal motivation works?
- Do you recognize other people's thinking styles and know what motivates them?
- When talking to groups do you lift your state and use language that increases effective communications?

The most complicated piece of equipment, comes with no instructions and performs in a different way every day – it's our people.

SIR TOM FARMER, CEO, KWIKFIT

RECOGNIZING PEOPLE'S THINKING STYLES

Why do people behave so differently? If you ask several people to do the same thing, why is it that one does exactly what you say, another wants to discuss it and find fault, or argues with you on each point, while a third person may completely ignore your request?

In a work situation, a supervisor may circulate a memo stating the compulsory manual-handling course is coming up and some people will claim they did not receive it. This is puzzling because these are the same few people who did not receive her carefully crafted missive about sending in annual leave forms a month in advance. What is happening here?

Types of thinking styles

Different people run different thinking styles. When the supervisor recognizes the styles those people are running, she will be able to make requests in ways that make it more likely that things get done, because the requests are addressed to staff in ways that meet their needs.

According to Fiona Beddoes-Jones, management consultant and creator of the training programme 'Thinking Styles', 'People who don't notice the small, to them unimportant things, may be "big chunk thinkers", interested in what we are going to do, not the minutiae of how we are going to get there. They might be people with a poorly developed mental filing system. Or they could be "mismatchers" – people who hate being told what to do.' As part of the programme, Fiona has developed a questionnaire that teaches staff first how to understand their own thinking style, then to apply it to other people's in order for them to learn to work together effectively as a team.

GETTING TEAMS TO WORK TOGETHER EFFECTIVELY

Shell and National Westminster Bank are already using 'Thinking Styles' to match jobs to the way people naturally process information. British Aerospace is using it to allocate tasks among teams of workers. Fiona says that 'When projects cost millions, anything that leads to team effectiveness and shortens the length of a job can potentially save huge amounts of money.'

Some people are visual and see pictures when they think. However, if you are an auditory person and hear what people say it may not occur to you that others take in information so differently. Fiona says 'Shut your eyes and listen to the words people use to engage with each other in your department. Someone who says, "I see what you mean" is thinking in pictures. To talk to them in their own language and find out if they understand your message, you might say "Do you get the picture?"'

'Some people are predominately intuitive. You can recognize their speech because they use words like "I feel we should do this". You will get more detailed information back from them if you ask how they "feel" about it.'

People also have styles of working with others. 'Matchers' are team people who like to work in harmony. They are good communicators and do well in customer relations jobs. Matchers are adaptive and tend to fit in with other people's wishes. They are not normally innovators, simply because they are too nice.

George Bernard Shaw said, 'The reasonable man adapts himself to the world. The unreasonable man persists in trying to adapt the world to him. This is why all change depends on the unreasonable man.' In a team the 'mismatcher' can be seen as the unreasonable person because they think new ideas through by disagreement.

'The first time you talk an idea through with a mismatcher', says Fiona, 'they usually disagree with you. But when you return they will have thought about it and be working towards an agreement.' Mismatchers make good computer hardware engineers because they will be acutely aware of all the possible risks involved.

We all use combinations of different thinking styles that can change depending on the task we are working on, how relaxed or stressed we feel and where we happen to be. The best type of thinker is a flexible one.

THINKING STYLES GRID

We use combinations of many different thinking styles but each style has traits. Some of the easiest types of thinkers to recognize are those who operate at the extreme ends of their scales.

Detail-conscious people notice small details. They take in information in small pieces as it relates to them.

Big chunk thinkers are able to assess a whole situation. They process larger pieces of information and key points. Big chunk thinkers are often leaders or responsible for major projects or strategies.

Procedural thinkers follow instructions and the accepted way of doing things. If you interrupt an extremely procedural thinker as he is explaining something, he may go back to the beginning and start to explain all over again.

Option thinkers want more choice in their work and to explore different possibilities. Easily bored.

Matchers like to conform, they are good team workers and communicators, and have a non-confrontational approach.

Mismatchers test an idea through disagreement. They often challenge the existing situation and are anxious for change.

Filters for sameness notice what is similar. They want stability and to find common ground.

Filters for difference notice if anything has changed or is different. At the extreme they can be faultfinders, good to have in your team for spotting errors but not to live with.

Processes for 'self' see situations in terms of their own needs and priorities and put themselves first.

Processes for 'others' put other people's needs first, above their own. Many people in the caring professions process for others.

Moving away from – some people avoid problems or threats by moving away from them.

Moving towards – some people, especially entrepreneurs, are really proactive, and off the scale for achieving their goals.

Reactive people respond to other people's requests or changes in situations or circumstances.

Proactive people initiate change, foresee problems and plan ahead.

Internally referenced people check how they are doing by asking themselves 'How am I doing?'. They go inside to check and are not dependent on other people's approval to know whether they have done something well.

Externally referenced people need others to tell them they have done a good job. They need praise and reassurance and rely on other people, supervisors, colleagues, friends and partners to tell them how they are doing.

Courtesy of Associated Newspapers, *London Evening Standard*, 'Just the Job'. Copyright Frances Coombes

Although people display patterns of behaviour that you can observe and sometimes predict, it does not mean that they will behave in the same way all the time. In fact, most of us have a capacity to surprise others.

Bosses and leaders are usually 'big picture' thinkers; they talk in generalizations, but they also tend to balance this by employing personal assistants that are detail conscious. Some people are flexible thinkers and function easily at either end of the thinking continuum; others can learn how to do it.

Managers who are cut off from the grassroots often depend on feedback from others about what is happening at shop floor level. The messages they receive will have been passed through the messenger's information-filtering system and selected according to what that person thinks is important to the employer. An employer who recognizes his assistant's thinking style can more easily recognize the type of information that he may not be getting.

Mis-matchers may be irritating, but they will tell you why your product launch will not work at the beginning, not at the end of your project. They will not wait to sympathize with everyone else when it becomes patently obvious why the plan did not work. Mis-matchers may not be the subtlest of communicators, but that is the price you pay for having an employee who is prepared to tell you the brutal truth at the start of a venture.

Flexible thinkers can change their habitual thought patterns at will and operate well at both ends of their thinking scale. For instance, a project manager may be a 'big chunk thinker' and able to visualize and have an overview of a major plan, say to build a hospital. She will also be good at breaking down the steps required for the outcome into procedural 'bite-sized chunks'. This type of flexible thinking helps her to clarify ideas and understand her role in situations so that she can feel reasonably sure beforehand whether the plan will work.

SHARING YOUR PEOPLE'S VIEW OF THE WORLD

People have preferential sensory systems – visual, auditory, and feelings, sensations or emotions – for the way they take in information from the world. You can build rapport with them by speaking in the same sensory language as they do. Using the same representation systems as other people builds rapport with them, and interrupting in another system will break rapport. It is good to know how to be in rapport, but it is also useful to know how to break it if you want to move a conversation along.

Educational consultant Cricket Kemp runs NLP northeast, a not-for-profit association which runs courses on teaching and learning skills for teachers. She says if you give people your message in their preferred style, they will learn and retain it better than if given in other modes. Studies carried out with children and adults and how they learn and take in information discovered the following.

🔊 **Pictures**. People who use predominately visual senses are often good at sorting for large amounts of information at a moment's notice. They may think in pictures and hold and rearrange information in a mind map.

🔊 **Words**. People who think in words find it difficult to hold information unless it is structured and the relationship is linear. They often use chants and mnemonics to remember things. Auditory is a good system for sorting known information, but is less useful for being creative.

🔊 **Feelings**. People whose dominant sense is feelings may need to physically do an exercise a couple of times before they get the hang of things. We retain much information in our body. If you have not ridden a bike for a long while and you sit on one, your body knows how to ride a bike even if you cannot remember. People who process through feelings, sensations and emotions are often very bright but may have never learned to process that information in a way that can be checked by others. Once triggered, this system will produce a mass of information at once, leading to a 'flash' of understanding.

If you want to communicate with everybody in this group you need to have pictures, diagrams and physical exercises that cater to all their representation systems.

Why do you need to know how people think and are motivated to do things? Here are some reasons why it is invaluable to know other people's thinking styles when you communicate with them:

- If you are a leader and need to motivate others, knowing how your people take in information and think will help you to communicate more effectively with them.

- When you know how your own internal motivation works, you can more easily understand other people's patterns and the best ways to guide and motivate them.

- If you understand more about the way people think, you can build rapport and have stronger relationships with clients, colleagues and friends on a deeper level than before.

- You can speak to groups of people using words that appeal to a range of thinking styles.

- You will become more capable of generating favourable or win-win solutions. If you can see more sides to a disagreement or problem, you are likely also to see more possibilities for solving them.

- If you are writing job adverts or advertising brochures and you want to appeal to a specific kind of reader, you can write in language that appeals to the thinking styles you seek in an applicant.

CONNECT WITH YOUR AUDIENCE

Much advertising is aimed at people who run an 'away from pain' strategy. The message about the penalties of not buying the right car insurance or of not having the right internet search engine is that if you do not do these things it will cause you pain. Yet that message may be largely ignored by the part of the population not hung up on the feel bad factor who quickly move away from heavy guilt trips. If the message is not packaged in a way that fits their criteria, those people will simply switch off and not notice it.

People filter incoming messages by selecting the parts they feel are relevant to them and that they expect to use later. They discard the rest.

How does an audience want you to communicate with them?

Your audience wants you to make them a promise and expects you to fulfil their expectations. They want you to use linked information, stories and jokes, and give handouts and exercises that will make your talk memorable. If you present your message so that it is appealing to several types of listener, you can ensure that everyone in your audience connects with and remembers what you said. If you are presenting to a general audience and you do not know their background, then:

- The biggest part of the population, 35 per cent, want to know 'why' they should listen to you. You have to win their hearts and minds and tell them at the start why what you have to say is important to them.

- Twenty-five per cent of your audience are thinking 'So what?' They want to know how useful whatever you are saying is to them.

- Just under one-quarter of your audience, 22 per cent, are wondering 'How do I apply this information? Show me how to use it.'

- And the remainder, 18 per cent, of the group are thinking 'What if' – 'What if I took this information and customized it, what does it mean to me and what can I do with it? What might it lead to?'

Source: statistics from Bernice McCarthy, author of the COLB Learning Styles book *The 4-Mat System* (Excel Inc., 1987)

If you are speaking to a group and you want to influence people, glance at your notes to see whether your talk will satisfy the sorts of questions that a general audience would want answered.

Progress now

An easy tip for increased focus while preparing a presentation is to cut out magazine pictures of people that represent your typical audience. Stick them on the wall and glance up at them as you write.

If you give each person in your pictures a name and then write the words, 'why?', 'what?', 'so what?' and 'how?' under each one, you can converse with each part of your audience individually at any brief sticking point. You can simply stop and say to 'so what?' – 'Well Dave, what did you think of the way I put that?' – and wait for the answer.

MANAGE YOUR STATE OF LEADERSHIP

If you are going to take somebody to a new or different level of understanding, you have got to go there yourself first. In order to convey information to a group of people, your energy level, state, motivation and enthusiasm must be higher than your audience's. It is your internal state and level of motivation that determine how well your talk will go. To connect to the group and to get them in a participatory mood:

🔊 Start by asking a question that requires people to raise their hands, for instance 'How many people are here today because they want to be?' To encourage them to do this, raise your own hand in the air when you ask the question and keep it there until you are ready for them to lower theirs.

🔊 Look at the people with their hands raised and briefly make eye contact with each of them. Then ask another question that will get the rest of the group to raise their hands: 'And how many people are here because they have been sent?'

🔊 Summarize what you have learned from the questions you have asked: 'It looks like 90 per cent of you are interested in the mating habits of the snail, so we are going to have a really interesting time tonight.' Glance round the room making eye contact again as you make this statement.

UNDERSTAND YOUR PEOPLE'S MOTIVATIONAL DRIVERS

Canadian Shelle Rose Charvet, author of *Words that Change Minds* (Kendall Hunt Publications, 1997), is one of the funniest and most knowledgeable international speakers on people's thinking styles. Shelle, who runs her language and behaviour workshops (LAB Profile) once a year in London through Frank Daniels Associates in Derbyshire, says: 'The better you understand someone's thinking strategies the more able you are to influence and predict their behaviour. If you are a team leader then you need to know which of your people are motivated by external circumstances, that is praise, rewards, recognition, and which are motivated by their internal beliefs and values.'

You can speak to groups of people using words that embrace a range of thinking styles, the main ones being for those who:

🔃 Run an 'away from' and a 'towards' strategy.

🔃 Sort for 'difference' and have a preference for 'sameness' at the same time.

🔃 There are also 'sameness with exception' people who like to hear words such as 'improvement', 'better, 'more' and 'less'.

People who move towards pleasure will tell you, 'Well, I saw this great job, it offered a lot of potential for me to do the sorts of things I wanted' and they will offer a list of criteria. People who move away from pain will say, 'Well, I couldn't stand my job any more, and so I left.' When it comes to partners, the story is similar: 'Well, I couldn't stand it any more so I got out.' The person who is motivated towards a goal might say: 'Well, I found a better partner, so I grabbed the chance to be happy.'

Do not assume that people who follow 'away from' strategies will do less well than those who run 'towards fulfilment'; both types can be phenomenally successful but are motivated towards their goals in different ways.

Where do your decisions come from?

Where in your body do you make decisions? Internally referenced people gather information from outside sources and then they decide about it, based on their internal standards. External people need other people's opinions to help them make up their mind. It is vital to know how you make decisions because it will determine the way in which you are motivated.

Progress now

You can find out how people make decisions by asking them 'How do you know when you have done a good job?' Ask this question of the next six people you meet, so that you get a selection of answers.

○ Some people will say: 'Oh, I just know when I've done a good job. It's a feeling.' These people are internally referenced and look inside themselves for the answers.

○ Others will say: 'I know I've done well when my supervisor/friends/ colleagues tell me I've done well.' These people are externally referenced and they seek confirmation from people outside.

○ Some people will say: 'Well, I suppose that really I know when I've done something well. But I like somebody to tell me so too.'

'AWAY' AND 'TOWARDS' PROBLEM SOLVING

How do the people around you react when confronted with problems?

- 'It's here so lets deal with it.' – Towards resolution.

- 'Oh no, not again, let's ignore it and see if it goes away.' – Away from pain.

These are extremes on the scale of reactions, but are generally how people think. People tend to follow patterns of behaviour in similar circumstances. Although you can often predict how they will behave in one situation, this does not necessarily mean they will run the same behaviour in another context.

Understanding other people's behaviour will let you know what motivates and triggers them to perform their best. Understanding your own habitual behaviour:

- Allows you to realize there are choices you can make and a variety of ways to do things.

- You do not have to keep repeating the same behaviour if it does not get the results you want.

TAKE CONTROL OF HOW YOU THINK

Suppose that you could record and store your own feelings and thought processes in a systematic way, using nothing more high tech than a pen and paper, you might say: 'What would I want to do that for?'

If it would enable you to compare past sensory blueprints of how you thought and felt and behaved during peak performances or when overcoming problems, and you could recall precisely what the triggers were that moved you on to greater heights – would that be interesting? Once recorded, you could review past scenarios and refine your future strategies, based on what you had learned, so that you would not have to repeat unproductive old behaviours any more – would this surprise you?

Until recently it has been mainly athletes and businesspeople, with the help of professional sports and personal achievement coaches, who have learned to record, store and refine their past sensory impressions in an amazing way that leads them to achieve world-class performances in their field.

Habitual thinking

The way you get out of bed in the morning, brush your teeth, or choose a partner are all habits you have formed. Try brushing your teeth with the other hand next time and see how different it feels initially. Most of us also think in habitual ways and there is a multi-billion global industry engaged in finding out how we think in order to get us to buy into ideas, beliefs or products.

When people are stressed, they often reconnect to past feelings of panic and dread experienced in childhood. It may be 20 years later and the person is a successful executive, but when faced with a deadline or a bigger challenge the old feelings of panic re-emerge that were felt when handing in a classroom essay and expecting to get bad marks.

That is why the facts that people give us during conversation are often less important than the sensory (seeing, hearing, feeling, smelling, tasting) language they use. Often it is the throwaway remarks, the ones we miss when listening to others, that hold most of the vital clues to their attitudes to stress or to bigger challenges.

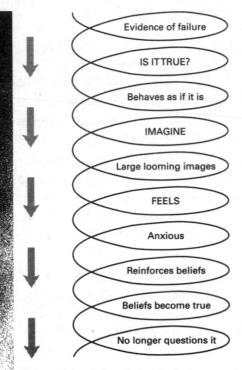

Figure 7.1 Downward spiral of a negative belief

CREATE YOUR OWN THINKING BLUEPRINT

Can you remember the last challenge you faced that you successfully solved? How were you experiencing the problem? What were you thinking seeing, hearing, feeling about the situation? What was stopping you from moving ahead?

By mapping your thought processes from previous challenging situations you can cut down the length of time spent agonizing at the same stage in the next encounter. If you already know that when faced with a new problem your initial reaction is usually one of: 'Oh no, I can't cope with this – I want to run away' (an '**Away from pain**' strategy) but that within a few days you rally and look for ways to turn the situation around, then you can shorten the process of problem solving by recognizing this and saying 'okay, what do I do next after I stop panicking? Oh yes, I start to look for a solution by generating **options**.'

Progress now

Jot down your thoughts and feelings about your last challenge sequentially from when you realized there was a problem until just after you felt it was resolved. Then take a highlighter pen and colour all the descriptive language you used to describe how you felt. Look at the thinking habits chart and mark an X along any of the continuum lines at the point you believe your phrases demonstrate that you were displaying a recognizable type of 'thinking behaviour'.

Thinking habits

The behaviours and attitudes that you run when you have problems.

 Necessity vs Options: If you found yourself thinking 'I have to do this' you are operating out of necessity. Try moving your thinking along the continuum line to the other extreme to see what new ideas are generated. Pause and think 'What are my options here?'

```
Necessity ———x———————————————?——— Options
SPECIFIC ———?—————————————————x——— GENERAL
Similar ————x————————————————?——— Different
EXTERNAL ——x—————————————————?——— INTERNAL
Away from ——x——————————————————?——— Towards
SELF ————x——————————————————————?— OTHER
```

🍃 **Specific vs General:** If you are thinking 'This always happens to me', you are generalizing. Asking yourself why is this specific thing is happening is a more useful question that will generate more answers.

🍃 **External vs Internal:** Is this a problem because I think it is, or because someone else has told me it is?

🍃 **Similar vs Different:** Is this problem similar to or different from other problems I've faced before? If so, how is it similar/different?

🍃 **Self vs Others:** Am I worried about the consequences for myself, other people, or both?

🍃 **Away from pain vs Towards pleasure:** Did I see this problem coming but put it off until it could no longer be avoided?

Now think about what happened to make you change your mind and decide that you could reach your goal. What changed in the above sights and sounds and feelings you were experiencing to help you achieve your outcome? Highlight those sensations in another colour and transfer to your blueprint.

Once you understand your own behaviour patterns around problems and how you solved them in the past you can record this information and let it work for you to propel you more quickly towards your goals.

Gill Shaw, NLP executive and brand coach of Fresh-look Experience, says: 'Beliefs are our driving principles which give us a sense of certainty, realism and direction particularly in decision-making. Positive beliefs are necessary to achieve our outcomes, and may even become our purpose. Beliefs work in conjunction with our values, which are the standards which frame how we live and provide the juice to motivate us.'

There are three parts to changing beliefs. You have to believe that:

1. **It's possible** – to be able to change a negative belief to a positive one you need to reframe and believe that it is possible to achieve (so that you can model success).

2. **You are able to do it** – that you are able to achieve it with the resources you have available, and that you deserve to achieve it. Otherwise you will have no commitment to your goal, or worse, you will sabotage your outcome because you don't believe you deserve the goal.

3. **Your goal is realistic** – you can change from a downward spiral of a limiting or negative belief, to an upward spiral of a positive belief when you know that something is possible because someone else has done it. Then it is possible for you to achieve if you believe you can do it.

- Reframe the context and content of your belief to a positive one.

- Substantiate your belief with evidence of past success.

- Act as if it is true.

- Reinforce your belief with ongoing evidence of success.

- Often when beliefs become true we tend not to question them and this can lead to inflexibility. In order to grow, you must constantly challenge your beliefs.

Beliefs, when charged with emotional intensity, become convictions and spur us to greater actions.

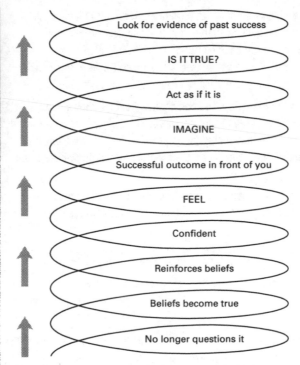

Figure 7.2   Upward spiral of a positive belief

SUMMARY

- If you are communicating with others and the outcome is important, make sure you recognize their thinking styles.

- When you present to groups of people, use language that increases effective communication.

- Look back at past problems and how you resolved them. Use the information you gain to create your own problem-solving blueprint to recognize your thinking processes around how you overcame difficulties in the past.

- Use your findings about your past behaviour around problem solving to speed up the actions that propel you towards future goals.

- Be aware of your internal values because the intensity of your beliefs fuels your motivation.

CHAPTER 8
Short Cuts to Success

- Do you know how to harness other people's success strategies and make them your own?
- Do you know how to stretch your thinking and stimulate your mind by modelling the habits of successful people?
- Do you know how to gather all the skills that you need to make your present situation and environment work for you?

The real art of discovery consists not in finding new lands but in seeing with new eyes.

MARCEL PROUST

There are a couple of universities around. There's Einstein's university you go to and you stand on the shoulders of others. Then there's the University of Life, and anyone who's been there has learned by his or her own mistakes. And that's okay, there's nothing wrong with that – it's just that it takes a hell of a lot of time.

There's a way of speeding up getting to where you want to go simply by looking at other people and seeing what works for them. When you really model other people it's not just a question of going to the 'experts'. If you've ever bought diet or healthy eating books, check out a picture of the author. Need I say any more about experts? There are questions about who and how we model. The mantra is 'adding to the choice we have.'

MARTIN GOODYER, MOTIVATIONAL TRAINER,
REACH INTERNATIONAL ASSOCIATES

MODELLING SUCCESS STRATEGIES

Success is seldom achieved by individuals working alone, it comes from working with others, entering their worlds, building relationships and recognizing the exceptional things that people do that work well and contribute to their success.

If you can figure out how another person can do something you want to do, it opens up a world full of possibilities. Knowing that you can observe, map and reproduce the strategies people use to become masters in their fields gives you a blueprint for success. You can model the skills of the most talented people around you and use these skills to achieve your personal goals and desires in life.

You might want to be thin, get promotion, be a better shopper, lover, businessperson, sportsperson, entrepreneur or host, you might want to do almost anything! Chapter 7 looked at habits and behaviour patterns that people display and *why* people do things; here we look at *how* they do them.

All professional athletes have coaches who teach them to notice and build on other successful sportspeople's strategies. Many of these strategies are also adapted and used in business to enhance people's team work, sales performance, negotiating or communication skills. Every franchise outlet that opens on a high street near you is modelled on the successful practices of businesses elsewhere.

You may not know what they are, but you also follow strategies for everything you do in life – from the way you comb you hair, do your shopping and decide what to eat when you are hungry. You run strategies for the things you do well, and also for the things you do badly.

NOTICE PEOPLE'S STRATEGIES

If you're in sales, human resources, training, or any business which requires advanced communication skills you can capitalize on the magic of understanding why people do the things they do. Get the action habit — you don't need to wait until conditions for learning new skills are perfect. Whenever you see somebody with a really good skill, one that you'd like to acquire, get into the habit of asking — 'How do you do that?'

How could knowing what motivates people to make their choice help you? You could try out successful people's strategies. Suppose you want to be slim, trim and active, you could model a range of slim people's thinking and behaviour and find out what it is about their strategies that keeps them slim. Ask them how they decide when it is time to eat.

Similarly, if you want to be a successful entrepreneur, spend an evening at an entrepreneur's gathering and build up a picture about what makes them different from the rest of the herd.

Arline Woutersz is President of the British Association of Women Entrepreneurs, affiliated to a World Association of 95,000 members. She says: 'Entrepreneurs are different because they are pro-active, they make decisions quickly and are also prepared to take the sort of risks other people might not.'

Entrepreneurs tend to think big and aim high. Arlene set up her first business when she was 35, using her home as collateral. Her latest business in a string of successful ventures is called Travel Health Solutions Ltd. The company takes people to South Africa for cosmetic and health treatments and afterwards on a safari holiday to recuperate. People go home from treatment looking healthy and tanned, they feel better and no one knows they had anything but a holiday.

What are the attributes of successful people?

- High achievers have a passion for what they are doing.
- Their goals are supported by their emotions.
- They believe their actions can make a difference.
- Life is about seizing chances and learning from experiences.
- The successful person's goal is overcoming challenges.
- They have the ability to observe, identify and adapt other people's strategies for their own uses.
- Their energy and enthusiasm comes from being on purpose and working towards their goals.
- Successful people are master communicators.

WHAT ARE YOUR ATTRIBUTES AND BELIEFS?

We have looked at how your beliefs, values, motivation and drivers influence what you believe you are good at or not good at and what you think you can and cannot do. Your beliefs about your capabilities leverage whether you achieve little or, like Superman, you burst through every obstacle and achieve a phenomenal amount. Stop and do a spot check on your beliefs now.

What are other people doing differently when they perform at their best? We will look at how modelling is used to train staff, how successful salespeople's skills are modelled, how to model, and the sorts of initial project some people have chosen to work on and why. We will also look at the results of a modelling project which was undertaken to find out what makes excellent teachers.

Progress now

Write down ten positive beliefs that you hold about yourself which have supported you, i.e. 'I'm a good . . .,' 'I will be successful because . . .,' 'I can do this . . . because.'

Now write down ten negative beliefs that you have held which have limited you, i.e. 'I'm not smart enough . . .', 'I'm not good enough . . .', 'I can't do it . . .'. Think about devising a simple modelling project which will provide you with the next step towards 'doing it', and repeatedly ask yourself 'what would happen if I could do it?'

Keep your list and throughout this chapter work on moving any items in the negative column to the positive. Systematically seek to improve your skills and performance capabilities and confidence in those areas.

When you start to model a new skill or behaviour, you should keep a note of the things you will *see*, *hear* and *feel* when you achieve your success. Chart your progress by consulting and updating your attributes list regularly to see which of your beliefs have moved columns.

MODELLING SUCCESS AT WORK

Do you know someone whose first job position was lower than the office cat's, and now they head an entire section? We have all seen it happen but can we ever hope to emulate it? If you think the person got there because they are brighter than you, have more qualifications, or managed to be in the right place at the right time, you may have mentally shut down all possible routes that could make you a success.

Ann Fuller-Good of training consultancy FOCUS Group runs workshops where management and staff discover what makes people excel at work. She says, 'If you want to be successful find a successful person and find out how they did it. If one person is good at a task because they have an interesting idea, that may not necessarily be a great way to do things. But if ten people have done the task in the same way, and they are all successful, you are getting close to excellence.'

Eurostar has used this successful blueprinting technique to train control staff who manage the rail terminals at Waterloo in London. Fuller-Good says, 'The aim was to find out what made excellent terminal controllers, and then give their colleagues the opportunity to try out the same thinking styles.'

Blueprinting excellence is more than taking on someone else's habits; you need to understand the beliefs that that person holds which make them outstanding. At workshops in other companies, Fuller-Good studied people who make excellent leaders and discovered that the overriding belief they held was 'There is more than one way of doing things.' She says, 'They believed that if they didn't get the result they wanted they could try a different approach. This belief manifested in the way they paid attention to achieving results.'

Fuller-Good states, 'If you're an admin person who would like to become a manager, then find someone who has the skills you'd like to be good at, say multi-tasking, or organizing things in chaotic situations. The questions to ask that person to bring out their underlying beliefs are: "How do you do this thing you're good at? And when you do it, what is important to you?"'

You may be in a position where you are expected to react to other people's needs, but if you want to become a manager you must become proactive. Imagine holding a successful manager's overriding beliefs for a day, such as: 'I can overcome all challenges.' Then notice the difference it makes to your thinking as an administrative worker.

Before adopting someone else's belief, it is important you choose it consciously, and practise holding it for a while. Ask yourself, 'How will holding this belief benefit me? Can I accept and feel comfortable with it?' If you can, then one of the best ways to make a belief your own is repetition. Stick the message somewhere prominent and repeat it ten times a day. It usually takes three weeks of repetition for a new belief to become embedded. Notice how quickly the belief begins to alter the way you think when dealing with work situations.

Are some people born with a success gene? Fuller-Good believes 'No, but some people have early life experiences that seem to motivate them to achieve more than others. These are people who believe they will be successful and work towards that vision. They don't fear failure, they see it as a challenge, and believe they will overcome all obstacles.

Is success worth the effort? You bet it is! Why not aim for it and see?

Courtesy of Associated Newspapers, *London Evening Standard*, 'Just the Job'. Copyright Frances Coombes

WHAT SORTS OF SKILLS DO YOU WANT?

What sorts of skills could you use that would motivate you and enhance your beliefs about your abilities, or advance your career and take you to the top? You do not have to reinvent the wheel and come up with totally original ideas. Start mining the attributes you see in the people around you.

GETTING STARTED – MODELLING A SKILL

Modelling other people's success skills and winning strategies will expand your potential to bring about similar successes. It will give you a deeper understanding of how people achieve excellence than textbook learning ever could. You also get new insight into the behaviour, beliefs, state of mind and sensory experiences that make up the whole experience when a person is engaged in the process that leads to their successful outcomes.

Begin to think:

- 📖 What sort of initial project would be most beneficial to you?
- 📖 What would possessing this skill say about you?
- 📖 What would it let you accomplish?
- 📖 What goal is this ability a stepping-stone to in your future?

The creative part of modelling requires you to stretch your thinking by taking on the beliefs, physiology and strategies of another person performing a skill you'd like to acquire and adapting it for your own uses.

CHOOSING A SKILL TO MODEL

Look around you — whatever environments you are in, there are bound to be people whose talents you admire and would like to acquire. Below are some examples of how patterning the successful way people do things has been used in the sales and education fields. Hopefully it will spark some ideas for your own new applications.

Some of the first skills that participants on a PPD Personal Development training company course modelled were: capturing the essence — the ability to simplify complex information; improved speed at mental arithmetic; the ability to assemble flat-pack furniture; making decisions in a timely manner; choosing the next move in a mountain climb; stopping mind-chatter and remaining focused; and establishing immediate credibility in a sales situation.

Modelling sales success

Understanding strategy is crucial for success in sales. Some sales people are instinctively good at selling but few can consistently generate new business. Consultant John Joint was asked by a large city firm to find a way to develop more people who could generate new business rather than just doing the sales. He says: 'For the modelling I talked to 15 people who already had this skill and learned some of the key factors about how they did it well. So we were looking at what were the successful people's drivers, what were their skills, what were the tools and techniques they used and what were their personal beliefs around what they were doing.

'We identified what the really good sales generators did that was different from other salespeople. And the key findings were that the motivation was not what people expected. Each person had a very strong driver that wasn't necessarily money or winning. It ranged from being interested in other people, to being interested in the subject, and it was the driver that motivated them to win, and they earned money as a result.'

Your models are all around you

Is there someone you know with a skill that you would like to model? One person might be a good organizer, another good at making quick decisions. You do not have to find someone who is a genius and excels at everything, only someone who excels in the activity you choose to model.

HOW TO MODEL

When modelling how other people do things, don't ask them 'Why' they do things, ask them 'How' do you do that?

🔖 Asking someone 'Why' he or she does something will get you a list of reasons, which may be well thought out or else spur of the moment answers to avoid feeling foolish because they don't know why they perform an action.

🔖 Asking people 'How' they do something is a cleaner way of questioning and does not impose on people's own model of the world. It will give you the person's *process* of how they do things.

Modelling a skill

Get the person to carry out or re-enact the behaviour, imagining they are actually doing, rather than observing, the task.

- Find out the very first thing the person is aware of as they enter the cycle of behaviour.

- Note which representation system they are using to enter the loop by listening for 'I see', 'I hear', 'I feel', 'I need to' . . . This will tell you the initial state the person needs to be in to start the process.

If they need to be prompted, ask:

- Did you see an image in your mind's eye?

- Did you say something to yourself like 'That's a job well done'?

- Did you have a feeling about it?

- Is the person triggered by something internal or external? Do they hear an inner voice, a memory or feeling?

Ask the person what they noticed next (picture, sound, feeling), and again identify the sensory representations. Keep asking the question 'Was there anything you were aware of before that?' until the person's description of their strategy appears. Carry on until you get the complete sequence of thoughts, pictures, feelings and actions the person runs to perform this task.

WHAT TO LOOK FOR WHEN MODELLING A SKILL

There are three things to look for when modelling someone's strategy:

1. What beliefs support the skill they are doing? Listen for words like 'I believe', 'I think', 'It's important that . . .'. These words indicate that whatever they say directly afterwards is important and it is what they believe about performing the task.

2. Pay attention to how their body language and demeanour change as they recount or run their strategy. Notice any change in their manner, posture and the way they hold themselves as they begin to relate their account and associate into the task.

3. Note at what point the strategy begins and ends. Once you have the person's strategy and know what makes them feel confident and competent about their abilities around it, you need to try on their beliefs.

Sit or stand as they did and adopt their body postures. Run through the strategy yourself saying it out loud as you perform it. Repeat whatever your model has shown and told you in precisely the same language they used. They will correct you if you are wrong because you have plucked this strategy from their world and the slightest mistake you make will jar with them.

At this point you have acquired the strategy. If you run it through and nothing happens for you, ask the person to do it again and talk it through because something may be missing. Sometimes when people are so familiar with a process that it becomes a habit there are parts of it that are so obvious to them that they fail to explain them. And the missing part is actually the most crucial piece of information that you need to have to make sense of how the strategy works.

Run through the strategy several times until you know you have it and then practise using it over a few days. Decide whether the beliefs that this person holds about performing the task fit well with your own beliefs before deciding to adopt their strategy.

Coding a strategy

So a tidy person's strategy might be that they first see an image of a tidy environment

🐾   which is a **visually constructed (Vc)** picture they imagine

🐾   this leads to a feeling, maybe of pride, pleasure, relief which is an inner feeling, which is **kinesthetic and internal (Ki)**

🕭 which may lead to the person thinking some internal dialogue, such as 'won't this place look brilliant when I'm finished' **auditory internal (Ai)**

🕭 and then the feeling **(Ki)** which motivates the action of performing the task.

So the code for that strategy is Vc, Ki, Ai, Ki – ACTION.

That person automatically runs the same strategy each time they tidy up because this is her habitual code for performing this action. When you can codify actions you can change very minute parts of the process later to find out what works best for you.

One benefit of codifying behaviour is that sometimes people who feel unconfident will run a strategy over and over again, a hundred or a thousand times, over a day a week or months before they finally take an action. A really skilled motivational trainer who works with that person can help them identify that part of their thinking and remove their looped behaviour patterns so that they take the actions that produce the results they want much more quickly than before.

CASE STUDY

MICHAEL BREEN

Michael Breen, Motivational Trainer and head of MBNLP, a training, coaching and consulting company, teaches participants on his NLP business practitioner course how to code their sensory images and thinking in order to see and remove the repetitive looped behaviour that many people engage in before they perform an action that makes them feel nervous.

'Managers may put off making difficult decisions. Salespeople may indulge in other behaviour to avoid making calls to customers where they feel their sales pitch may be rejected. For many participants, once they see their own behaviour coded on a flipchart they say "Oh yes, that's exactly what I do and that's where my time goes!"

'Once people recognize the unproductive energy-sapping behaviour they indulge in, they can often change their habits within a few minutes by practising and removing the loops.' Michael Breen goes on, 'Then I say "Now what are you going to do with all that extra time you have saved by identifying your unproductive behaviour loops and removing them from your life?" And that really motivates people to keep the new, less stressful, more time-saving, behaviour going.'

Eye assessing cues

People tend to look up when they are making pictures in their head. They look down when they are experiencing feelings and remembering past events. They may look from side to side when they are hearing sounds. They may even hang their head to one side so they hear better in one ear. You can communicate better with people when you know how they filter and take in the information.

Progress now

You can hone your skills at observing eye assessing cues by watching TV quiz games. First note the type of question asked, then which quadrant the contestant immediately moves their eyes to in order to access the information.

If you were modelling how to be a successful salesperson, how to do a successful interview or how to chat up someone on a date, knowing this type of information gives you an indication of whether the person is listening to what you say. It also indicates how they are processing the information: in pictures, sounds or feelings. If they are mostly looking up and use visual descriptions, and you paint your ideas in pictures, you will be talking their language and building rapport with them.

Where do people locate types of information?

If people are pointing and waving their hands around in front of you as they talk, begin to notice where they locate certain types of information. If you ask them 'Where is the past?', they might point and tell you it is behind them. If you ask 'Where is the future?', they might point and tell you it is in front of them.

What can you do if you know where people locate different sorts of information? Imagine you are a salesperson and you want to sell a customer your brand of computer, but they have another type in mind. While the customer describes the computer they want, they may look and point at a space in front of them. This is the place where they store their picture of their ideal product. The salesperson spots the ideal product location and may wave his hands around in that area as if to disperse the existing image and then make movements of pushing the rival computer off to one side. He then starts talking about his company's product, and placing it neatly in the customer's 'ideal product' space. You will see some salespeople who know where customers locate their 'new purchase space' and use this subconsciously.

ACQUIRING A STRATEGY

If you are a disorganized person and you would like to be tidier, find a tidy, organized person who agrees to let you model them. Tidy people tend to be organized in their minds about where they store information. If you ask them a question such as 'What colour is your front door?', they may look up to their left, a common place where people hold their visually remembered images. If you ask them 'What would a melon look like if it sprouted legs and turned into a caterpillar?', they might look upward and to the right where they construct their visual images, because they would have to make that picture up before they could imagine it.

People tend to be consistent about where they store types of images and information, and organized people usually hold a model in their heads of what 'tidy' looks like. They have a good storing and sorting system for placing and retrieving things.

If you ask someone who does not have an organized retrieval system about how they store information and images, 'What is the colour of your front door?', their eyes may dart all around the place, up, down, round and round, as if they are searching for the location of the information. If you ask them 'What does tidy look like?', they may tell you that they cannot imagine it, or that an image of untidy may dart through their mind first. By modelling and practising the precise sensory, eye assessing cues and thinking strategy of the organized person, the messy person can begin to bring order to their world within a very short period of time. Sometimes the person just says 'Oh, I get it!' and it can happen within 15 minutes.

MODELLING SKILLS IN TEACHING AND LEARNING

Cricket Kemp, trainer, of Learning Excellence says, 'We tend to see and teach from our own model of the world. Teachers tend to teach in their own dominant sensory profiles (often visual), and may not understand enough about how someone who is auditory or kinesthetic takes in or stores information to be able to adapt their teaching methods to meet a child's learning needs.

'To help a child who is auditory and is having difficulty with spelling you have to put your own model away in order to understand their world and how they perceive it and develop strategies that will work for them. While learning a list of words rote fashion may help a child spell these words, it does not make them a good speller or increase their capability to spell. Good spellers tend to repeat an automatic internal visual process to spell a word correctly.

'We're hoping to tackle problems like this by bringing an understanding of neuro-linguistic programming (NLP) into education and modelling how people who do things well do those things. We need to understand the thought processes and beliefs that a person holds and be able to incorporate it into our repertoire of thinking styles in order to understand it and teach it to children who use predominately non-visual representation systems and who are often left behind in education.'

Children who are predominantly auditory (hear words, then spell them) or kinesthetic (able to feel that a word is correct) are distinctly disadvantaged in a visual learning setting, so we teach them a visual spelling strategy.

   Visual learners — may hold their pictures in 3-D mind maps, and find it very easy to rearrange information around in them.

🔁 **Auditory learners** – may find it difficult to hold information unless it arrives in a structured way and the relationship is linear. If I want to do my accounts I do them in auditory, and I will have them laid out in an ordered fashion. It is a good system for sorting known information – not good for being creative.

🔁 **Kinesthetic learners** – are often bright but have not learned to translate the information they hold to a form that a teacher can mark. It's a system where there are triggers that will give you a lot of information in halting and sporadic bursts, which may initially be confusing.

Visually dominant people may appear brighter than the others because they speak quicker. Their reactions may be quicker and they can access and sort through their picture information quicker than others. But once those doing visual processing recognize the patterns and connectivity between things they may switch off and stop looking for further clues.

The other groups may make significant breakthroughs through flashes of insight and leaps in understanding where they can move in an instant from not knowing to knowing how to do something. (Einstein made many of his leaps in understanding

Progress now

Poor spellers who are auditory or kinesthetic may be slower at learning because they often mouth the words as they read in an attempt to understand a spelling.

Change to a visual strategy . . . Learn the process . . . can spell

If the task you are tackling is not going as well as you would like it to do, then choose someone else's strategy for doing it. If what you are doing isn't working then try something else.

in a flash.) This type of kinesthetic learner may seem slow to learn yet at times demonstrate that they are very bright which can be confusing or irritating for teachers.

Kemp says: 'We are encouraging children to switch between sensory representation systems to perform different tasks. So if I have a whole bunch of information how do I make sense of it? Visual is a good system to be in to view and arrange the information, and then maybe to structure it you want to switch to auditory and write it down.'

MODELLING GOOD TEACHERS

The people modelled were teachers recommended by heads of staff, other teachers and pupils as exceptionally good at teaching. They were all very different types of people. The similarity patterns noticed were:

- Language. Good teachers never said 'Stop talking.' They said 'Listen to your colleagues, they might be saying something important and you need to listen to me so that you know how to do the exercise.' Every instruction was about how the person should be, and it was never ever 'Stop' or 'Don't' or other negative words.

- Model of the world. When asked what model the teachers had in their head, they said it was of a perfect lesson. Where the children were on their best behaviour and were all learning well, all working and talking to each other in appropriate voices. Holding this model of how things are in your head gives you the language to tell people what to do. You are telling them what is in your mind and not looking around for children doing bad things. The teachers were directing them to act in a positive way.

- The teachers treated everyone fairly and complimented everyone fairly. The children knew what to expect.

🔖 The teachers were very knowledgeable about the subjects. The children said that the material was broken down in a way that if they asked questions no one made them feel they were stupid. The teachers explained things in a different way if people did not understand, whereas other teachers would say it louder, as if you had a hearing problem.

🔖 Three of the teachers said similar things: 'We break the teaching down and make it simple, but we *don't* water it down. We are teaching children the proper material at the right level.' They did not make the work easier for the children, they just made it easier to learn.

🔖 The teachers also demanded respect, for themselves and for *all* the pupils. The children would say, 'They are really friendly but you always know they are the teacher.' They treated the children with respect and pupils were not allowed to laugh at other children in class.

Cricket Kemp concludes that 'Great teachers in learning and in life pass on the way they are experiencing and patterning the world. They teach you "how" they know, not what they know. They engage your senses in the subject, and widen the patterning you do. The very best of them teach you how to go on widening your patterning through the future.'

There are many ideas here to get you thinking about planning your own strategies for achieving your purpose. Look at all the ideas and ask yourself 'How could I adapt that for my uses?' Take the modelling projects mentioned in this chapter and brainstorm 20 ways you could adapt some of them to further your aims.

Two of the most powerful tools you have in your armoury are your 'To do' list and your 'modelling skills' abilities. You cannot control the future or decide what you will be doing five years from now when success knocks on your door, but you can decide on the next small steps you will take today and tomorrow to make the success you want a reality. Get motivated – start increasing your skills and taking the actions that make successes happen more quickly.

SUMMARY

- ⓑ Get into the habit of trying on other people's strategies for achieving successful outcomes.

- ⓑ Know your purpose and design a plan of action to acquire the talents and abilities you need.

- ⓑ Notice good models of success strategies and stretch your thinking about how you might adapt them to achieve your own goals.

CHAPTER 9
Getting Time on Your Side

    Where do you keep time in relation to
    goal setting?

    How far ahead is your next major triumph
    'in time' planned, and can you bring it
    nearer?

    Are you 'in time', 'through time', 'behind
    time' or are you left wondering what has
    happened to the time?

Time, like a snowflake, slips away, whilst you
are deciding what to do with it.

ST LOUIS BUGLE

You do not use time, it uses you. Whether you race to complete tasks as quickly as possible or you sit at a desk and do nothing at all – time still passes at the same rate and you cannot have any of it back. However, what if you could strike a balance and complete more things, more of the time?

Time does not fly. It does not drag by. We have a relationship with time – one we can change for the better. Wendy Sullivan of Discovery Works Limited, an in-house workforce trainer, says: 'If you need better time management skills, the solution is not actually about "managing" time because time cannot be managed. Time just "is". The question is how you choose to manage yourself in relation to time. People do things for one of three reasons:

- They are drawn to the task and want to do it.
- They have no choice, they must do it.
- They do things that allow them to put off what they most want to avoid.

Then afterwards they may feel guilty, frustrated or resentful about the way they've apportioned their time.'

Time management techniques do help us to take more short cuts, stop wasting time and become more productive. But it is possible to have an even better relationship with time by knowing how you think about it in relation to your work. Are there periods when time 'drags'? Or do you see time 'flying by', only noticing and possibly regretting it when it has gone. Knowing how you relate to time and listening to what you say to yourself about it is the first step to understanding why you do things the way you do. It also gives you an option to change how you think about time.

HOW DO YOU DO TIME?

Answers to the following questions will vary if you change the context to work, home or social situations, so choose one context. Tick a box on the left OR right for each item.

Are you often surprised by how much time has passed when you look at your watch?	Do you usually know the time to within a few minutes?
Is your diary filled with loose papers all ready to fall out?	Is your diary well organized and tidy?
Do you ignore deadlines others give you and avoid setting deadlines for yourself?	Do you set yourself deadlines and treat them as important?
Do you delay making decisions so that you can be flexible and keep your options open?	Do you like to make decisions well in advance?
Can you easily focus on what you are doing so that everything else is blocked out?	Do you find it difficult to concentrate when you are in a hectic environment?

Do you get caught up in what is happening so that you forget about other things you need to do?	Do you automatically keep track of things while involved in something else?
When you talk with someone is it usually the other person who ends the conversation because you are so involved in it you do not realize it is time to stop talking?	Are you often the one to end a conversation?
Do you prefer to be spontaneous?	Do you prefer to plan beforehand?
Do you sometimes arrive late without realizing that you are late?	Do you usually arrive on time and know if you are even a few minutes later than the agreed time?
Do deadlines seem to creep up on you without you noticing?	Are you aware of deadlines moving slowly closer to you from a long way off?

🔖 If you ticked six or more boxes on the right, you probably live life in an organized, methodical way. If you want to become more flexible, ask yourself 'What will happen if I do not know what is planned?'

🔖 If you ticked six or more boxes on the left, you probably lead a flexible life with minimum forward planning. You may end up rushing to get things done or feel guilty about things that you have not done.

🔖 If you ticked a mixture of boxes you may be someone who is flexible when managing yourself in relation to time – congratulations.

Courtesy of Associated Newspapers, *London Evening Standard*.
Copyright Frances Coombes

WHAT IS YOUR RELATIONSHIP WITH TIME?

And how do you make time work for you?

- Are you 'in time' and live for the moment and 'right now'?

- Are you 'through time' and plan each moment, and know precisely where you will be and what you will be doing in ten years' time?

- Are you 'behind time', remembering the past and how different things are now?

- Do you live 'in the future' at some joyous point where everything will be wonderful, but shut down on now?

- Are you drifting through life as a casual observer, or did you just wake up one day and wonder 'what has happened to all your time'?

Progress now

List the types of tasks you are doing:

☐ When you notice you have 'too much' time.

☐ When you experience 'too little' time.

☐ When you say to yourself, 'It's just the right amount' of time.

WE ALL DO TIME DIFFERENTLY

People may clear out clutter on two levels:

🐾 One on an *environmental level*, the office, files, computer software no longer needed, which is now encroaching space.

🐾 The second set of decluttering is on a *time level*. This may be due to procrastination by you or the people around you who waste your time.

A visible mess in a cluttered office, kitchen or house is easier to organize than a cluttered time schedule. Because time is invisible and there may be no messy piles of papers lying around as evidence, people who eat into large portions of your time unnecessarily often take longer to detect and deal with. However, organizing time is not that different from organizing your office environment.

DISORGANIZED SPACE – DISORGANIZED TIME

Disorganized space	Disorganized time
Untidy drawers	Cluttered time schedules
Lack of space	Lack of thinking time
Excess baggage	More tasks than time to do them
Items jammed into any space	Tasks moved because of lateness

Solution

One solution for 'through timers' who need to work with 'in timers' is to explain when you meet people that your time is very important to you. 'In timers' may not understand what the fuss is about, so give a couple of examples of the sort of behaviour you want to see. For instance, 'I expect people to turn up on time and give as much prior notification as possible if they need to change meetings so that I can schedule something more productive to do with my time.' If they are still not responding then move on to explaining your beliefs about other people and time, such as 'I believe that people who do not turn up on time are not showing respect for me', or 'are stealing my time'.

If you are a person who has to work with a space invader or time invader, think about the behaviour they are demonstrating and the types of things that might be influencing the situation. If you cannot take control of your paperwork or time schedule then ask these questions of yourself.

Is the problem:

- An environment problem – 'Where is it happening?'
- A person's behaviour – 'What are they doing?'
- Your capabilities to manage your time or space – 'How'?
- Your beliefs and values – 'Why'?
- Identity – 'Who'?
- Part of the system – 'Who else' or 'What else affects it?'

Be aware of the invisibles – beliefs, values and identity

The table overleaf shows the route by which we change our thinking when we change our beliefs. If you start at the bottom with 'environment' and work upwards to 'identity', you will notice that while environment, behaviour and, to some degree, capabilities can be seen, beliefs, values and identity are largely unseen. However they are there and can be detected.

If you choose to make any permanent changes in your environment clutter or want to use your time more effectively and your decision is to be a permanent one, you will need to think it through and make a change in your thinking at a beliefs level.

Identity	**Who?**	
Beliefs and values	**Why?** Does it fit with your beliefs?	Is this a belief that you hold about clutter? Perhaps you do not know how to deal with it the way other people do.
Capabilities	**How?** How capable are you to deal with it?	Is this a skills and capabilities issue? Have you been trained to deal with clutter?

| Behaviour | **What?** What type of behaviour displays the problem? | What is the problem? Someone else's behaviour/ your own/ the result of both? How is the behaviour manifesting itself? |
| Environment | **Where?** Business, home, the location? | Where is the problem? Your surroundings/head/both? |

Adaped from Robert Dilts *et al*, *Neurological Levels of Thinking*

QUESTION PEOPLE'S ASSUMPTIONS ABOUT TIME
Time lines

Progress now

Ask a group of people to explain to you how they perceive time. Ask each one to stand in the middle of a large room or outside in a clear space and:

🔾 Point to where they locate 'the past'. They may turn round and point behind them. Some people see time as a straight line that runs from behind them, through them and straight out in front of them.

🔾 Then ask them to point to where they see the future. They may point to somewhere in front of them. However, others hold feelings of time differently, they may sense time around them or through them, and others construct time as a circle. There are all sorts of alternative ways that people do time. Ask a roomful of people to point one finger to their past and another to their future and to hold the poise. You will be amazed at how differently they all see time.

Mike Treasure, a physicist and NLP trainer, says: 'If you are going to solve a problem with time, your own or other people's, you need to have an overview map of how individuals think of time.'

A systematic way to find out how someone considers time is to ask them to pick a location and stand where they want their 'now' to be located. Then ask them to point and walk to where they see their past and future.

By getting people to walk along their time continuum and explain their thinking about how they will complete a difficult task at various points, you can achieve a sense of how they perceive the problem in relation to time.

SORT OUT YOUR COMPLETION DRIVE

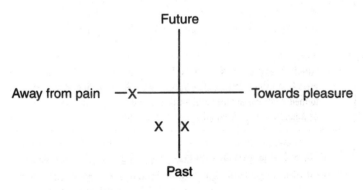

This is a very simple feelings-based exercise, and you really need to just do it, rather than read or think about it too much. You will get an instinctive realization instantly as you stand on different parts of your time line.

- Find a large clear space and write the words 'Moving away from', 'Moving towards', 'Future' and 'Past' on large sheets of paper.

- Stand where you consider yourself to be in relation to the problem. This might be 'I want to ask for a raise', 'change my job', 'I want to take on more business', 'go for a really big contract' or 'I want to ask someone for a date', 'I want to write a book'. Then place the sheets of paper on the ground in the places you feel represent your past, future, towards pleasure and away from pain.

- Stand on your 'now' at a place where you feel most comfortable in relation to 'time' and the 'pain' and 'pleasure' of achieving your goal. Think about the challenge you want to undertake and close your eyes and breath deeply. As you do so, notice any thoughts and feelings you are experiencing.

- Step outside your model for a moment and move to the edge of the room. You may even want to stand on a chair to look down and get another view of where you chose to stand in relation to 'time' and 'pain and pleasure'. Looking down on the situation, are you surprised at where you positioned yourself?

- Now step back onto your model to where you feel most comfortable on the 'Away from pain – Towards pleasure' line. Are you standing closer to one extreme than the other? Notice what you think and feel about yourself in relation to the project.

- Now move along your thinking style line a little at a time, towards the other extreme of thinking that you normally shy away from when planning ahead. Describe what you feel as you get closer to the other extreme. It may be uncomfortable standing closer to pleasure if you habitually motivate yourself with pain. Nevertheless, describe out loud what you are feeling and any new insights you have received from imagining the pleasure of the successful completion, and the celebration and recognition that comes with it.

- Notice what you are feeling about the project as you stand at different points.

- Then do the same moving along the 'Past' and 'Future' line.

- Experiment with where you stand and what you feel at different points on your model. Notice and carry back all the extra information and insights you have collected about your future undertaking.

This type of exercise releases information on the reasons why you might be feeling anxious or blocked, and also offers unexpected solutions for overcoming obstacles.

PROCRASTINATION – THE ART OF KEEPING UP WITH YESTERDAY

Procrastinators will go to great lengths to convince themselves and those around them that they are engaged in productive activities, while avoiding the main task they want to achieve. They are often frustrated people who never realize their aims or potential. Although procrastinators can make excellent critics and may help you tremendously by telling you where you went wrong and how to improve your work, lifestyle, romance, finances or weight loss, they may not make much headway in these departments themselves.

When pressed for results, procrastinators will assure you they know that the deadline for completion is the weekend, but they have many other important tasks competing for their time. They just have one or two more details to collect. They need to speak to a couple more people, and play an extra game of tennis this afternoon because exercise is really important for them when they are under pressure.

When a procrastinator says they have a great idea and wants to talk to you about it, one way to stop them in their tracks is to say 'Great, go and work out a plan. Then come back to me with something on paper that we can both look at.' If they are a real procrastinator, nothing will happen after that because the procrastinator's time line stretches only as far as thinking, not as far as doing. Success is doing, not wishing.

Perfectionists

There are many reasons why people do not produce results on time. Perfectionists cannot let go of anything until it is perfect. A deadline comes and goes and the task is completed days later – perfectly.

CHOOSE A BETTER APPROACH TO TIME
Can't prioritize

The important task looks daunting, so some people do other smaller tasks, but do not make much headway with the most important part of the project. Inability to prioritize can also be a 'time' problem if you are an 'in time' person and have no sense of how time passes in relation to getting things done.

Break your workload into small chunks

Making lists that prioritize tasks and which move you forward each day can help. Assign a level of importance to each task you do:

🖎 **Urgent.** Your immediate tasks that must be done now in order to make things happen in the future.

🖎 **Important.** The things you are setting up to happen next.

🖎 **To do.** The regular things you must do around tasks and events to make things happen: book a room for an event, thank a speaker, check a date.

🖎 **Note.** Things that are coming up in the future that you need to be aware of, and maybe gather information and prepare for.

SENSE TIME MOVING

Deal with things straight away

An invitation to an awards ceremony arises. Decide whether to go or not. Make a decision about what you intend to do and deal with that piece of paper straight away.

Follow your natural rhythm cycle

Notice how you perform at different times of the day and fit your tasks around your natural rhythms of working. If you are best in the mornings, attack the big tasks then and leave letter opening and phoning people to later in the day.

Things that go wrong are not disasters

Analyse what happened and what, if anything, you could have done to save the day. Work out a plan of how you might do things differently to get a different result, and file it away for future reference. In all areas of life disappointments sometimes precede success. 'It's not a crime to make a mistake', Walter Wriston, former chairman of Citicorp once said. 'What is a crime is failure to learn from a mistake.' If what you are doing is not working, try something else.

223

Focus

When situations are moving quickly it is sometimes difficult to gauge what is actually happening. At times like this, the best thing may be to stand back and become detached from the situation. Ask yourself, 'What is at stake here?', 'What is important?', 'What will matter in ten years' time?' Imagine you are an alien and see things and ask questions from a different point of view.

Get sorted

Finally, find some organized people and model their strategies in relation to time and clutter. Take what you have learned from modelling successful time and space users and use their strategies to perform one small clutter-clearing task.

- Resolve to do this task really well and complete within a realistic time frame.

- Take some time to celebrate and feel really good about your achievement.

Progress now

Wendy Sullivan advises: 'Discover the things that are really important to you by asking yourself as you perform each task, 'How will doing this help me achieve my goal in life?' Now choose some of the new time strategies you have learned that reflect the way you would like to operate.

- If you are a perfectionist, drop your standards. If you wait until things are perfect you may never finish tasks.

- Do the important stuff first.

- Practise saying 'No'. Just because you can do something does not mean you have to do it.

- It takes a lot of time to procrastinate, so stop doing it. One way is to change your self-talk from 'I should' to 'I'd like to finish this by . . .'

- Make decisions more quickly. Ask a few good decision makers how they do it and practise for best results.

SUMMARY

- Find out how you do time in relation to goal setting.

- Learn how to handle people who have different relationships to time.

- Organize your time the way good planners organize their physical clutter.

- Sort out your completion drive.

- Problem solve by bringing future time closer.

CHAPTER 10
Pulling It All Together

- Are you committed to being successful at whatever you do and are you prepared to raise your standards in order to get it?

- Do you have an unshakeable belief that you can get whatever you set out to achieve in life?

- Are you mentally equipped with the tools and problem-solving techniques you need to deal with any challenges?

- Are you flexible enough to tailor your strategies to get the results you desire?

- In short, do you know what to do, the order you need to do it in, and how to apply your whole focus to achieving your goals?

**You are your own Devil, you are your own God.
You fashioned the paths your footsteps have
trod.**

TIEME RANAPIRI, A MAORI POET

**Regret for the things we did can be tempered
by time; it is regret for the things we did not do
that is inconsolable.**

SYDNEY J. HARRIS

You have reached the part of the book where you may start to
wonder, 'Well, what did I get out of that?' This book was designed
to motivate you if you wanted to move from just thinking about
the things you would like to achieve to actually doing them. Are
you on your way to designing your personal action plan for
creating the future you want, aided by the tools, tips and
techniques you have acquired to help you become more
motivated?

RECAP

If you filled in your motivational skills wheel in Chapter 1, you already have an insight into how you fare in relation to many of the skills that highly motivated people possess. You may have analysed your weak points and have been pleasantly surprised by some of your strengths.

Many of the skills we have looked at are ones found in leaders and senior managers. In addition, leaders are often noted for their ability to live with ambiguity; they can make plans and move forward without having every part of the jigsaw present. They also tend to have good listening skills which enable them to absorb a great deal of information quickly, and pick out the significant points from what people are saying.

HOW WELL DO YOU LISTEN?

Paul Burns, Organizational Development Consultant and Psychotherapist, uses the Psychology of Mind (POM) method to show how most of us think while listening to others. 'First, we listen at a high level to understand what the person is talking about, then our listening level drops as we begin to think about the implications and applications around what they have said. Gradually our attention drops below the level of listening, to "I agree/disagree with what you are saying". We may interrupt at this point to do a comparison and say "Here is my story". After that we drop to nodding politely and not listening.'

Much of what we learn from other people when we talk to them does not come from listening to the actual words they use; we sense it with our whole being. In studies done at the University of Texas to assess personality traits of 2,000 managers, it was found that, without exception, senior executives scored higher than middle managers when it came to thinking intuitively. Part of what is termed intuition comes from people's ability to listen and take in information in ways which may seem magical to other people who do not possess the same degree of listening skills.

Progress now

Practise listening

Spend five minutes listening to a friend recounting an experience. Your job is to listen, just nodding and keeping the conversation going by asking them questions if they dry up.

🔁 Now go back and run through the conversation in your mind and think about what was happening with you as you were listening to that person.

🔁 Did you stay focused on what they were saying? Or did your attention slip through these different levels of listening?

Psychology of Mind (POM)

LEVELS OF LISTENING

UNDERSTANDING

Engaged in understanding what is being said.

IMPLICATION

Thinking about the implications.

APPLICATION

Thinking about the applications of what has been said.

NOT LISTENING
AGREE/DISAGREE

Where you are thinking 'I agree/disagree with what you are saying'.

'HERE IS MY STORY'

At this point you interrupt to tell your story.

NOT LISTENING

By this point you are nodding politely and not listening.

Progress now

Decide before the next conversation you have with someone that you are going to listen to this person in an understanding way, then see how easy or difficult this is for you.

TYPES OF LISTENING

There are different types of listening:

🕲 **Random thinking.** Where thoughts come into our heads, similar to internal dialogue.

🕲 **Process thinking.** A learned way of thinking where we sort and evaluate, using past memories for comparison.

🕲 **Flow Mode.** Comes from a clear mind. The depth of thought is variable and it may appear random but it is not.

Flow mode is the best style to be in when you are listening to other people; you are relaxed and trust that the information you want will come.

A challenge

🕲 Can you control the way in which you choose to listen to another person for a full five-minute period?

🕲 Or does your listening just happen for you?

QUANTUM LISTENING

On his 'Living Inside Out on Purpose' workshops, Michael Mallows, life coach and workshop facilitator, teaches quantum listening skills. He says that 'Many people who ask questions think that they already know the answer, so they are seeking confirmation not information. Or they are not really asking the question, they are telling the answer, such as: "Have you spoken to him about that?" which means you should speak to him about that. And so, even when listening, we have this urge to tell, to instruct, to rescue, to know better.

'Quantum listening is listening at every level, paying attention to what's happening inside us, maybe noticing that our stomach is a bit tense. You're paying attention to your internal self-talk and what is happening around you. You check out your assumptions but you allow the intuitive process to happen and you notice any subtleties.'

Listening to yourself

Make a stream of consciousness recording into a tape recorder by talking out loud. Just say whatever comes into your head and notice how random and non-sequential your thoughts are. Doing this a few times makes you aware of the internal chatter inside you, which can make it difficult to listen attentively to other people.

Listening to others

If you have the urge to interrupt someone, make sure that the interruption is preceded by a recap by saying: 'Let me just check I'm understanding' or 'Let me just recap on what I have understood you to say', rather than jumping in. This gives the person a chance to say 'No, I didn't say that', and it gives you a chance to reflect. It also lets people know that even if you are going to interrupt and counter what they have said, you have heard and understood them and are including them in your thinking process.

ALIGN YOUR BELIEFS AND VALUES

When the actions and behaviours we take support our deepest needs and we are free from internal conflict, we produce our most magical results. Once you know what excites and motivates you, and you are prepared to take the actions to make your dreams a reality, then you will magically move towards your purpose.

Now you need a procedure for standing back and scrutinizing your ideas to know whether the goals you seek are attainable, and what period of time they can be achieved in (Chapters 2, 4 and 9).

Success means different things to different people. Someone else might see success as having the energy, fitness and body of an athlete, another person might see success as creating something unique, having a millionaire lifestyle or a loving relationship. Another person might see their success as helping others and making a difference to people's lives. However you define your success, you need to make a plan and put an order to it.

YOUR GOALS SHOULD BE SMART

🔃 Define your goals within the context of your values (Chapter 3).

🔃 There will always be some things that you might want if there is little effort involved, but when the going gets tough you drop them in favour of goals that are more meaningful to you.

🔃 Always produce a well-formed outcome on every project you intend to start. Rank your goals by level of importance to you. Make sure that you are not deflecting your energy by focusing on too many goals. Some will be distractions that will never come to fruition, but they will divert some of your attention from the things you really do want to achieve (Chapter 4).

🔃 Listening skills — ultimately your goals will be achieved with the help of other people, so develop good communication, persuasion and listening skills.

FOLLOW YOUR PASSIONS

What do you feel passionate about? What do you burn to do? What would you do if money was no object and you could do anything in the world you wanted to do?

Progress now

Pick one big, perhaps scary, enormous and great idea that you yearn to achieve. You may have been nursing your idea for a while but never thought it through completely.

◊ Allow yourself the luxury of spending a week thinking about this big idea and just letting it grow and grow. Do not put boundaries around your thinking – let the ideas build and explode in your mind. Keep a notebook to write your ideas down – do not censor anything.

◊ Go back a week later as a realist and spend some more time asking, what would have to happen for these ideas to work for me?

◊ Comb through your ideas picking out the nuggets and discarding the sludge. You may have come up with a completely different idea by now and have moved on to something more realistic. That is how many people make great leaps towards achieving the things they have always wanted to do.

WHEN CREATING IDEAS

◊ First comes the dreamer – you ask yourself questions such as 'What would I do if I had no restrictions?'

◊ Then the realist – 'How can I make it work?'

◊ Finally the pragmatist – 'Is this a good idea?', 'Who would want it?', 'Who's done it before?', 'How can I test it out?'

THE MOTIVATIONAL SKILLS WHEEL

Below are some of the main skills that successful people either have or work hard to achieve.

1. Motivating yourself and others to do things.

2. Visualization. Imagination and rehearsing your dreams of the future and how it will look, feel and taste when you achieve it. Harnessing the power of emotions.

3. Feeling purposeful. Do you know enough about your beliefs and values and how to anchor them securely to your purpose?

4. Goal setting. Do you know how to create well-formed outcomes? Have you learned the 21-day habit to regularly achieving your goals?

5. Getting rid of limiting beliefs that hold you back from being truly successful.

6. Training. Do you know the areas you need to acquire more skills in? Are you constantly developing new skills?

7. Communication. How good are you at understanding your own and other people's thinking styles when there is a need for motivation?

8. Modelling. Do you know how to model other people's skills in order to get the results you want?

9. Time management. How good are you at working within time frames. Are you 'in time', 'through time' or 'behind time'?

10. Pulling it all together. Have you used your newly acquired skills in real-life situations, adjusting and smoothly pulling strategies together so that they can work at peak efficiency for you?

Imagine again that each spoke of the wheel represents a skill or ability that you value and want to become even more accomplished at. How do you rate your level of competency under each of the headings on a scale of 1 to 10 now? Number 1 represents the middle of the wheel and 10 the outer rim. Again draw a dot on each of the spokes at the competency level you think you presently operate at in each of the ten skills. Do not think about it, just do it quickly.

When you compare it with the original motivational wheel you filled in (Chapter 1, page 26), have you scored higher at any of the competencies? Have you learned anything new or surprising about yourself and your particular strengths? Has your confidence or competency grown in any of the areas covered? This is really what motivation is about – building competencies, knowing yourself and what you really want, and having the confidence to act upon your dreams.

Figure 10.1   The motivational wheel

WHAT IS YOUR NEXT ACTION?

Are there any areas in your motivational wheel chart you need to improve on? If so, you could concentrate for a week on one area at a time, say increasing your goal-setting abilities, or banishing limiting beliefs, or finding and modelling other people's strategies that work. Could you devote your efforts for a week to simply becoming more purposeful and increasing your motivational drives, or enhancing your performance?

Do you believe that you could raise your standards and become 10 per cent or even 20 per cent better at any of the topics covered? Of course you could! We can all become better in any areas we focus our attention on.

The motivation wheel gives you an 'at a glance' overview of your perceived competencies – it is your blueprint for success. The trick is to know the order in which to do things so that you can become systematically more powerful in your thinking, action planning and completion drives.

GATHERING YOUR RESOURCES

Remember when you did something well, something that made you feel really proud? What were the beliefs you held then about your abilities to achieve your aim, and what sorts of things did you say to yourself about what you were doing? Was your motivation drive high? Recall that feeling and harness it.

Remember, in everything that is really important to us – love, life, friendship, caring, success – feelings come first. We may spend our school life learning about logic, but all the really big decisions we make in life, such as whom we marry, where we live and what we want from life, are made with our emotions. Martin Goodyer, motivational trainer of Reach International Associates, says:

'The feelings come before the actions. Therefore you need to be finely attuned to your feelings. When your feelings and whole attention are focused on your goal, you can attain it, provided you know the syntax for success – which is the order of how you do things.'

YOUR ACTION PLAN FOR SUCCESS

1. **Raise your standards**. Whatever your standard is now, whether good or bad, it is not relevant, it just is. Whatever you have in life you have got everything you deserve because the actions you have taken to date have produced it. These are the standards that you have set for yourself until now, and until you do something different you will not get a different result. Only when you raise that standard yourself can you expect to raise your expectations.

2. **Have an unshakeable belief**. Raising your standards is not enough. You need to have an absolutely unshakeable belief that says 'I know I can do it'. If you do not have that you will get a little voice in your head that says 'Who are you kidding?', 'You've never done it before', 'Why are you going to do it now?', 'What makes you think you're going to do it now?'

3. **Banish your devil**. The voice in your head is like a little devil that follows you around. You have to banish the little devil, or at least dumbfound him so that he has nothing to say.

4. **Know what to do and apply it**. Remember a time when you were able to do things that you did not think you could do before? Where did you find the references for doing these things successfully? Look around you now and when you see people with skills you would like to acquire, ask them 'How did you do that?'

When you find simple strategies that will work, collect them and use them. There is a way of doing most things and you need to have a simple strategy that gives you the order for the process to work. While there is nothing new in this world, when we do things in a very specific order, we can create magical results.

Your purpose and destiny are intertwined. As your thoughts, plans and actions flow together, your energy grows because you are doing what you love doing. Now you are focused on creating the outcomes you want. You have the tools, you have the motivation, you feel powerful – take the next steps and journey towards your biggest goals.

> Don't be afraid to take big steps. You can't cross a chasm in two small jumps.
>
> DAVID LLOYD GEORGE

Motivational Trainers

Fiona Beddoes-Jones of BDJ Associates runs a series of thinking profile courses. Telephone: 01476 861010.

Michael Breen heads MBNLP, a training, coaching and consultancy company delivering NLP and business programmes to individuals and companies worldwide. He has worked with Richard Bandler and has revolutionized the design and delivery of NLP training in the UK. Website: www.mbnlp.com or telephone 0870 11 62657.

Shelle Rose Charvet, international sales and HR motivational trainer and author of *Words that Change Minds* (Kendall/Hunt Publishing Co., 1995). She is based in Canada and delivers training in England through Frank Daniels Associates. Email: info@frankdanielsassociates.co.uk.

Pete Cohen, sports coach and TV and workshop motivational trainer, runs Lighten Up weight loss programmes. Website: www. Lightenup.co.uk.

Frances Coombes, journalist and motivational trainer in career and personal development skills. Workshops include 'The Escape

Kit – exploring career changes and beyond' and 'Make Something Happen!' – spend a day working out your route to success. Email: FrancesCoombes@Yahoo.com or telephone 0207 609 1617.

Dave Crisp is managing director of PPD Personal Development, one of the largest NLP training companies in England with some of the best known speakers in the NLP world. Website: www.ppdpd.co.uk.

Ann Fuller-Good of training consultancy FOCUS Group runs workshops for management and staff. FOCUS Group: 020 8543 2288.

Martin Goodyer, motivational trainer of Reach International Associates, runs Reach4Success motivation days designed to 'whoop 'em up' and get people motivated. Designed to cover all the main aspects that people are likely to want to succeed in, each part having an expert motivational speaker in that area – finance, health, fitness, confidence, fun and putting it all together. Website: www.reach4reach.com.

Ideas UK are an ideas and staff recognition scheme association. Savings made from employees' bright ideas submitted to schemes in 2001–2002 are forecast to generate £500 million pounds over the next three years. Website: www.ideasUK.com.

Cricket Kemp, Training Consultant and Educational Adviser of NLP North East and Learning Excellence, runs NLP training workshops, trainer trainings and magic spelling days for children, teachers and adult non-spellers. Email: nlpnortheast@patterning.demon.co.uk.

Greg Levoy, motivational speaker, author of *Callings – Finding and Following an Authentic Life* (Three Rivers Press, New York, 1997). Delivers workshops in England through Heart at Work. Website: www.heartatwork.net.

Michael Mallows, life coach and workshop facilitator, runs 'Living Inside Out on Purpose' workshops and teaches quantum listening, effectiveness training and other self-development skills. Website: www.mallows.co.uk.

Alex McMillan, sales trainer and founder of the 100K Club for Top Sales Performers, author of Q Learning: *Entrepreneur* (Hodder and Stoughton, 2003). Email: alex@successmoves.com.

Gill Shaw, NLP executive and brand coach of Fresh-Look Experience, is a life coach. Website: www.fresh-look-experience.com.

Wendy Sullivan of Discovery Works is an independent workforce trainer in time management, values etc. Telephone: 020 8400 4832.

Peter Thomson, entrepreneur and motivational speaker, Peter Thomson International Plc. Website: www.peterthomson.com.

Mike Treasure, teacher, NLP trainer, and physicist, has an unusual approach to problem solving in relation to time. He also runs workshops on joined-up NLP, or how the whole of NLP joins together. E-mail: mike@jtreasure.demon.co.uk.

Simon Treselyan of Starfire is an international motivational trainer who deals with the physical aspects of motivational training, the firewalk etc. Website: www.starfire-world.com.

Nick Williams, motivational speaker, Director of the Heart at Work Project, and author of *Unconditional Success* (Bantum Press, 2002). Website: www.heartatwork.net.

Andrew Wood, President of Ideas Management, based in Washington and UK and editor of Ideas Express, also PRISM computer software, a specially tailored Ideas Management system for generating staff ideas in large organizations. Free copy online at www.ideasmanagement.com.

Helpful Books

Steve and Connirae Andreas, *Change Your Mind – and Keep the Change*, Real People Press, 1987.

Richard Bandler, *Using your Brain for a Change*, Real People Press, 1981.

Richard Bandler and John Grinder, *The Structure of Magic Vol. 1*, Science and Behaviour Books, 1975.

Richard Bandler and John Grinder, *Frogs into Princes*, Eden Grove Editions, 1990.

Leslie Cameron-Bandler, David Gordon and Michael Lebeau, *The Emprint Method*, Future Pace, 1985.

Robert Dilts, *Changing Belief Systems with NLP*, Meta Publications, 1990.

Robert Dilts, Tim Hallborn and Suzy Smith, *Beliefs*, Metamorphous Press, 1994.

Genie Z. Laborde, *Influencing with Integrity*, Syntony Publishing, 1987.

Anthony Robbins, *Awaken The Giant Within*, Simon and Schuster, 1992.

John Seymour and Joseph O'Connor, *Introducing Neuro-Linguistic Programming*, Harper Collins, 1993.

NOTES

NOTES

NOTES

NOTES

NOTES

NOTES

NOTES

NOTES

NOTES